Phonics *Plus* B

Student Edition

John F. Savage, EdD

Professor Emeritus
Lynch School of Education
Boston College

Consultants

Francine R. Johnston, EdD
University of North Carolina at Greensboro
Phonics and Phonological Awareness

Melanie R. Kuhn, PhD
Rutgers University
Fluency

Melinda S. Rice, PhD
Elon University
Comprehension

Cindy A. Strickland, MA
University of Virginia
Differentiated Instruction

Illustrator

Anthony Lewis

EDUCATORS PUBLISHING SERVICE
Cambridge and Toronto

Acquisitions/Development: Kate Moltz
Senior Editor: Stacey Nichols Kim
Senior Editorial Manager: Sheila Neylon

Senior Designer: Heather L. Terry
Cover Design: David Parra
Typesetting: Bob Doron and Sarah Rakitin

ISBN 0-8388-1021-4

Printed in U.S.A.

1 2 3 4 5 QWD 09 08 07 06 05

Contents

Unit 1

iii

Unit 3

Parent Letter

Dear Parents,

Second grade is an important year for your child. In second grade, children become more independent and gain more skills that will help them become good readers and writers.

The work your child will be doing in this book of *Phonics Plus* builds on the work he or she has done earlier in the program. Your child will continue to learn about the sounds of the English language, how to sound out new words they meet when they read, how to read words they couldn't read before, and how to understand and enjoy stories that people have loved for generations.

Your involvement in helping your child learn to read and write remains as important as ever. Some of the pages your child will bring home from this book have activities on them for you to do together. These activities are at the bottom of the page, marked with this symbol 📖. Help your child practice new skills by doing these fun, simple exercises together.

You can also promote and support learning at home by:

- *Reading with your child every day.* Read the stories that are too hard for your child to read, and have him or her read to you the stories that can be read independently.

- *Building new vocabulary.* Point out new words in stories and poems. Think of different words to express ideas: How many words can you think of that mean the same as *quiet*? Don't be afraid to use new words when you talk to your child.

- *Helping your child sound out new words.* As you shop at the supermarket or at the mall, help your child sound out words like *clearance* and *asparagus*.

- *Asking your child about school.* Praise your child's best efforts and proudly display the work that your child brings home.

Learning doesn't stop when your child leaves school every day. What you do at home remains a very important part of your child's development as a reader and a writer.

Sincerely,

John F. Savage

Carta a los Padres

Queridos padres:

El segundo grado es un año muy importante para su hijo/hija. En el segundo grado, los niños se vuelven más independientes y adquieren más destrezas que les ayudarán a desarrollar sus habilidades lectoras y escritoras.

El trabajo que su hijo/hija llevará a cabo con el libro *Phonics Plus* refuerza el realizado con anterioridad en el programa. Su hijo/hija seguirá aprendiendo los sonidos del idioma inglés, cómo pronunciar las palabras nuevas que salen en las lecturas, cómo leer las palabras que antes no podían leer, y cómo comprender y disfrutar con los cuentos que encantaron a generaciones enteras de personas.

Su participación en el desarrollo de las habilidades lectoras y escritoras de su hijo/hija sigue siendo tan importante como siempre. Algunas páginas de este libro que traerá a casa contienen actividades para que las realicen juntos/as. Estas actividades se encuentran en la parte inferior de la página y están indicadas con este símbolo 📖. Ayúdele a su hijo/hija a practicar nuevas destrezas haciendo estos divertidos y sencillos ejercicios juntos/as.

Otras formas de estimular y apoyar el aprendizaje en casa son:

- *Leyendo con su hijo/hija cada día.* Léale cuentos que son demasiado difíciles para él/ella, y haga que él/ella le lea los cuentos que ya puede leer por su cuenta.

- *Enriqueciendo su vocabulario.* Señale las palabras nuevas que aparezcan en cuentos y poemas. Piensen en palabras distintas para expresar la misma idea: ¿Cuántas palabras se te ocurren que signifiquen lo mismo que *callado*? No tenga miedo de utilizar palabras nuevas cuando hable con su hijo/hija.

- *Ayudándole a su hijo/hija a pronunciar las palabras nuevas.* Cuando estén comprando en el supermercado o en el centro comercial, ayúdele a pronunciar palabras como *clearance* y *asparagus*.

- *Pidiéndole a su hijo/hija que le explique lo que hace en la escuela.* Elogie sus esfuerzos y exhiba con orgullo los trabajos que traiga a casa.

El aprendizaje no se detiene cuando su hijo/hija sale de la escuela cada tarde. Las actividades que lleven a cabo en casa son una parte muy importante del desarrollo de sus habilidades lectoras y escritoras.

Atentamente,

John F. Savage

Meet Two Friends

Read about Mike and Cate. List three things you learn about them.

Mike and Cate

Meet Mike and Cate. They are friends. They are in second grade at the Apple Hill School. Their teacher is Mr. Chen.

Mike and Cate live in the city. Mike has a little brother named Matt. Cate has a cat named Puffy and a goldfish named Goldie.

Mike loves to play soccer. Cate likes to ice skate. They both like dinosaurs and they both love to read and tell stories.

Mike told his little brother Matt a funny story. You can read it on the next page.

Three things I learned about Mike and Cate:

1. _____

2. _____

3. _____

Soup from Stones

> **Read this story. Why is it funny?**
> **Talk about the questions.**

Two men walked into a town. They had not eaten in days. They were very hungry. They knocked on a door. A woman came to the door.

"We are very hungry," the two men told her.

"I have very little food," the old woman replied. "Only some potatoes."

"Potatoes!" the men shouted. "What luck! We have two stones. We can use your potatoes to make soup with our stones. Bring us a pot of water."

The woman brought the two men a pot of water. They lit a fire and boiled the water. They dropped their smooth stones into the water. The woman added the potatoes.

A neighbor came out of his house to see what was going on. "We are making soup from stones," the old woman said.

"I can add some carrots," said the neighbor. He dropped some carrots into the pot.

More neighbors came to see what was going on. They added peas, beans, and onions. They added tomatoes and other vegetables. Finally, the soup was ready.

All the people ate a big, delicious meal. And the men left the village with their bellies full.

Think & Talk

How did the people in the town help the men?
How did the men help the people in the town?

Say each picture's name. Write the first letter of each animal's name. Color those letters on the keyboard.

1.

___ orse

2.

___ ig

3.

___ ow

4.

___ uck

5.

___ amb

6.

___ oat

 Brainstorm some other animal names with your child. Have your child point to the letters on the keyboard as he or she spells the names aloud.

Name _____

Initial Consonant Sounds: Zoo Animals

 Say each picture's name. Write the first letter of each animal's name. Color those letters on the keyboard.

1.

___ion

2.

___iger

3.

___ebra

4.

___onkey

5.

___iraffe

6.

___angaroo

q w e r t y u i o p
a s d f g h j k l
z x c v b n m

 Brainstorm more animal names that begin with *l, t, z, m, g,* and *k.* See how many you and your child can come up with for each letter.

Read the sentences. Draw a line to connect each sentence to the picture it describes.

1. Ann and Al are angry. ● ●

2. Uncle Ug puts up his umbrella. ● ●

3. Iggy is in the igloo. ● ●

4. Ed Elephant has an egg. ● ●

5. Ollie Ostrich sings opera. ● ●

Name _____

Review Initial Sounds

 Say each picture's name. Write the word for each picture. Then write the name of the story that the letters in the shaded boxes spell.

S	U	N				
O						
U						
P						

F		
R		
O		
M		

S					
T					
O					
N					
E					
S					

_____

_____

_____

Final Consonant Sounds

 Say each picture's name. Circle the three pictures in each row whose names end with the same sound. Write the letter that spells that sound.

1.

_____
_ _ _ _ _ _
_____

2.

_____
_ _ _ _ _ _
_____

3.

_____
_ _ _ _ _ _
_____

4.

_____
_ _ _ _ _ _
_____

Final Consonant Sounds

 Say each picture's name. Circle the three pictures in each row whose names end with the same sound. Write the letter that spells that sound.

1.

    _ _ _ _ _ _ _

2.

    _ _ _ _ _ _ _

3.

   _ _ _ _ _ _ _

4.

   _ _ _ _ _ _ _

Draw a line from each ball to the basket where the letters belong, then write the missing letters in each word.

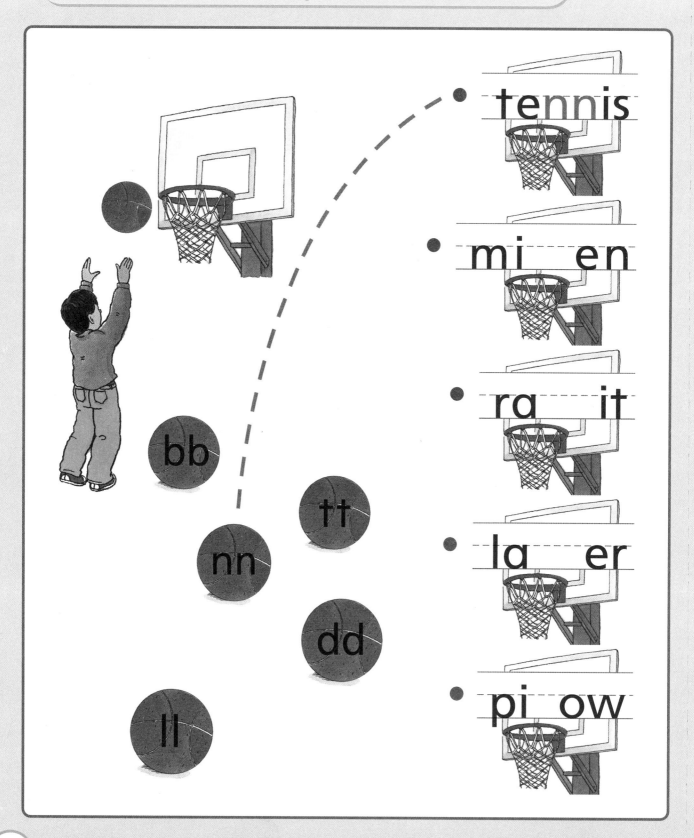

Medial Consonants

Draw a line from each ball to the basket where the letters belong, then write the missing letters in each word.

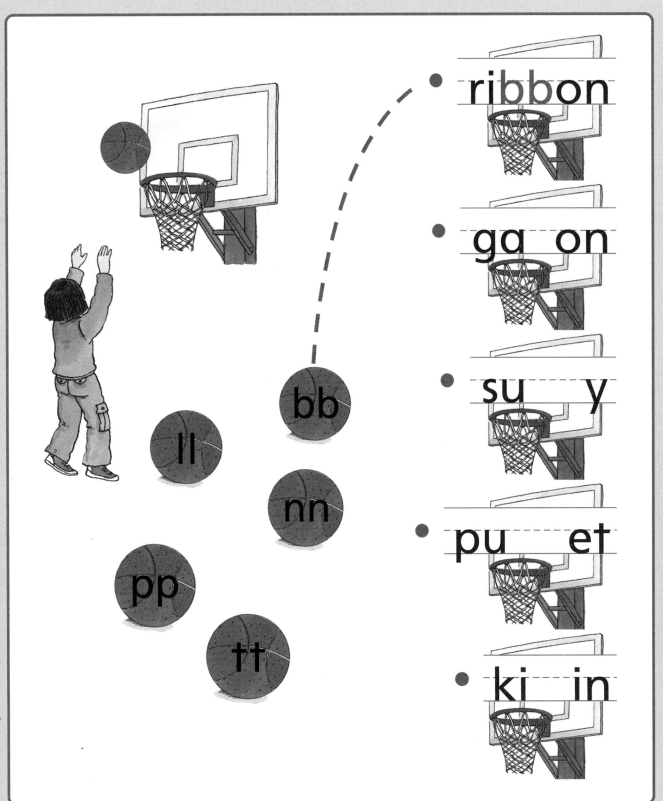

ribbon

ga __ on

su __ y

pu __ et

ki __ in

Medial Consonants

Syllable Step-Down

 Say each picture's name. Write the syllables for each word in the boxes. Follow the example.

1.

umbrella

| um |
| um | brel |
| um | brel | la |

2.

octopus

| oc |

3.

elephant

| | |
| | | phant |

4.

alligator

| | | ga |

Star Words: *said, should, have, love*

 Read the Star Words. Fill in the blanks with Star Words. You will use one word twice.

said   **should**   **have**   **love**

1. "Please come to my birthday party," _____ Gail.

2. "You _____ be there at three o'clock."

3. "We will _____ games and food."

4. "I would _____ to go," I told Gail.

5. "What _____ I bring?"

Lesson 7b   15

Two Sounds of c

Circle the cat if the picture's name starts with a hard c sound. Circle the city if the picture's name starts with the soft c sound.

Reminder
The letter c has two sounds. It has a hard sound in words like **cat** and **cot**. It has a soft sound in words like **city** and **cent**.

1.

2.

3.

4.

5.

6.

7.

8.

9.

Name _____

Two Sounds of g

▶ Circle the goat if the picture's name starts with a hard *g* sound. Circle the giraffe if the picture's name starts with the soft *g* sound.

1.

2.

3.

4.

5.

6.

Read the words in the box. Then sort the words by word family. Write the words on the lines.

bug	hug	page	rage
cage	lace	place	tug
face	mug	race	wage

-ug

<u>bug</u>

_____

_____

_____

_____

-age

_____

_____

_____

_____

_____

_____

-ace

_____

_____

_____

_____

_____

_____

Writing Sentences with g-Words

> Read the words in the boxes. Write the words on the lines to complete each sentence.

| giraffe | stage | giant |

The **giraffe** is on the _____ _____.

| Ginny | gate | big |

_____ is at a _____ _____.

| gum | get | bag |

I can _____ some _____ in a _____.

| goose | page | goofy |

The _____ _____ is on the _____.

Say each picture's name. Circle the letters that make the sound at the beginning of each word.

1.

ch sh th (wh)

2.

ch sh th wh

3.

ch sh th wh

4.

ch sh th wh

5.

ch sh th wh

6.

ch sh th wh

7.

ch sh th wh

8.

ch sh th wh

9.

ch sh th wh

10.

ch sh th wh

11.

ch sh th wh

12.

ch sh th wh

Writing Initial Consonant Digraphs

 Read each sentence. Write the missing letters on the lines.

| sh | ch | th | wh |

1. I like to sit in the blue _____ **air** .

2. Simon tried to catch a _____ **ale** .

3. Do you _____ **ink** you can make soup

from stones?

4. One, two, buckle my _____ **oe** .

5. Jack can _____ **op** down the beanstalk.

6. The mouse took the _____ **eese** .

Writing Initial Consonant Digraphs

Write the digraph *wr* under the pictures.
Read the words you make.

Reminder
At the beginning of words,
wr has the sound of r, such
as in **wrist** and **wrap**.

1.

_____ite

2.

_____ist

3.

_____ench

4.

_____eath

 Read the words in the box. Write
the best word in each sentence.

| wrap   wrote   wrong   wren |

1. A _____ is a small songbird.

2. I will _____ the gift.

3. It is _____ to do bad things.

4. Mr. Wright _____ me a letter.

Initial Consonant Digraphs *kn* and *gn*

Reminder
At the beginning of words, the digraph **kn** represents the n sound in words like know and knob.

▶ **Write the digraph *kn* under the pictures. Read the words you make.**

1.

_____
__ ot

2.

_____
__ ob

3.

_____
__ ee

4.

_____
__ ife

▶ **Read the words below the pictures. Write the best word in each sentence.**

gnat   gnu   gnome

_____
- - - - - - -

1. A big _____ was at the zoo.

_____
- - - - - - -

2. I could not see the little _____.

_____
- - - - - - -

3. I read a story about a garden _____.

Review Initial Consonant Digraphs

 Read this silly limerick. Circle all the words that begin with *kn* and *gn*.

A knight that I know from Peru
Got a gift of a very large gnu.
   It was in a bad mood
    And it ate the knight's food.
So he sent his new gnu to the zoo.

 Find all the words that begin with *kn* and *gn*. Draw a line through each word. Write the words on the lines.

knight	knit	knife	knee	gnu	knock	know

K	N	I	G	H	T
N	B	K	N	I	T
I	F	O	U	C	Q
F	K	N	E	E	V
E	H	K	N	O	W
G	K	N	O	C	K

_____ _____ _____ _____

_____ _____ _____

Name _____

Homophones

> Read the words and definitions in the box. Circle the
> word that completes each sentence. Write it on the line.

---

no: opposite of yes
know: being aware

right: opposite of left; opposite of wrong
write: to use a pen or pencil to record ideas

knot: a lump formed by combining two strings
not: a word used to say *no*

night: opposite of day
knight: a royal servant

new: opposite of old
gnu: an animal that looks like an ox

---

1. Ben got a _____ cap.   (new)   gnu

2. When the sun goes down, _____ comes.   knight   night

3. Can you _____ me a letter?   right   write

4. Please do _____ walk on the street.   not   knot

5. Do you _____ Sal?   no   know

Star Words

⭐ this ⭐ that ⭐ where ⭐ there ⭐ then ⭐ when ⭐ these ⭐ those

1. _____   5. _____

2. _____   6. _____

3. _____   7. _____

4. _____   8. _____

 Underline the Star Words in each sentence.

1. This is my hat. That is his hat.

2. Where is the swing? Oh, there it is!

3. When we get on the bus, then we will leave.

4. These trees are pretty. Those are not.

 With your child, tell a story that uses these Star Words. Take turns adding sentences to the story.

I Lost My Cap

Mike and Cate love this poem. Read it. Underline all the Star Words from page 26 as you read.

I lost my cap,
I don't know where.

I think I see it
Over there.

I lost my coat,
I lost my hat.

I'll find them soon
Just think of that.

I lost my sock
And that's not fun!

I found a sock.
Is this the one?

I had ten socks,
I lost all ten.

I'll find some now,
I'll find some then.

I think I'm losing
All my clothes.

Don't worry,
I can find all those.

I lost my pencil
And my pen.

I'll get them back,
I'll tell you when.

I really don't know
What to do.

Don't worry.
I'll take care of you.

The Man Who Sold Hats

 Mike and Cate love this story. It takes place in Africa. Read it. Talk about the question.

Once upon a time there was a man who sold hats. He made hats of many colors: red, blue, green, and black. On market day, he would put all his hats on his head and go to the village to sell them.

One day, on the way to the market, the man got tired from carrying so many hats on his head. He sat under a tree by the side of the road. He fell asleep.

When he woke up, his hats were gone. He only had one hat left, the hat on his head.

"Where are my hats?" the man yelled. "Someone stole my hats!"

When he looked up, he saw that the tree was full of monkeys. And on every monkey's head was a new hat. "Those are my hats," the man said. "Give me back my hats," he shouted. The man stamped his feet. All the monkeys stamped their feet.

The man waved his arms and shouted louder. "Give me back my hats!" The monkeys waved their arms.

The man jumped up and down and yelled even louder, "Give me back my hats!" The monkeys jumped up and down.

At last, the man took off his hat and threw it on the ground. The monkeys took off their hats and threw them on the ground.

The man picked up all the hats, put them back on his head, and went to the market.

Think & Talk What would you have done if you were the man?

Have your child read this story to you. Talk about the question at the end together.

Final Consonant Digraphs: *sh, ch, th, ck, ng*

 Say each picture's name. Circle the letters that make the sound at the end of the word.

1. 	2. 	3.
(sh) ch th ck ng	sh ch th ck ng	sh ch th ck ng

 Read the words in the box. Write the best word in each sentence.

> **back   beach   flash   sick   sing   wish   with**

1. My dog has a spot on his _____.

2. I _____ I could _____ as well as Ben.

3. We saw a big _____ in the sky during the storm.

4. Ming and Lee will go to the _____ to swim.

5. Come _____ me to the party.

6. Carlos is _____ today.

Word Families with Final Consonant Digraphs

 Read the words in the diamond. Sort the words by word family. Write the words on the lines.

-ash

_____

_____

_____

_____

-each

_____

_____

_____

_____

bash

beach   bring

cash   dash   dock

king   lock   mash   peach

ring   reach   rock

sing   sock

teach

-ing

_____

_____

_____

_____

-ock

_____

_____

_____

_____

Consonant Digraph *ph*

Reminder

The digraph **ph** represents the **f** sound in words like **phonics** and **photo**.

> Write the digraph *ph* under the pictures.
> Read the words you make.

1. 	2. a b c d e f g h i j k l m n o p q r s t u v w x y z	3. 
_____ one	al_____abet	ele_____ant

> Read the words in the box. Write
> the best word in each sentence.

autograph   alphabet   elephants   phone   trophy   photo

1. Ralph won a _____ for the race.

2. Lee called Ina on the _____ .

3. I love to see the _____ in the zoo.

4. My little sister knows the _____ .

5. Here's a _____ of Mike and Cate.

6. I asked the soccer player for her _____ .

Name _____

Review Initial and Final Consonant Digraphs

Say each picture's name. Fill in the letters at the end of the word. Read the words you make.

1.  bru___	2.  ___eel	3.  ___one
4.  pea___	5.  ___ree	6.  fi___
7.  tee___	8.  ki___	9.  ___eese

 Ask your child to read the words on this page to you, then make up a sentence using each of the words.

Initial Consonant Blends with *l* and *r*: *fl-, tr-, pl-, gr-, bl-, br-, gl-, dr-, sl-, cr-, cl-*

 Say each picture's name. Circle the letters that make the sounds at the beginning of the word.

1. (fl) fr tr

2. pl gr gl

3. sl cl pr

4. bl br gl

5. pr dr sl

6. br tr br

7. cl fr cr

8. gr gl sl

9. bl pl br

10. cr tr cl

11. fr fl sl

12. br dr tr

Name _____

Writing Initial Consonant Blends with *l* and *r*

 Say each picture's name. Write the letters that make the sounds at the beginning of the word.

| cl | br | fr | tr | dr | bl |

1. ___ **friend**	2.  ___ **iff**	3. ___ **ash**
4.  ___ **ack**	5. ___ **um**	6.  ___ **ick**

Read these clues. Write the missing letters. Read the words.

1. another word for thin ___ **im**

2. a dark color ___ **ack**

3. what I do to water or milk ___ **ink**

4. what I do when I'm happy ___ **in**

Say each picture's name. Circle the letters that make the sounds at the beginning of the word.

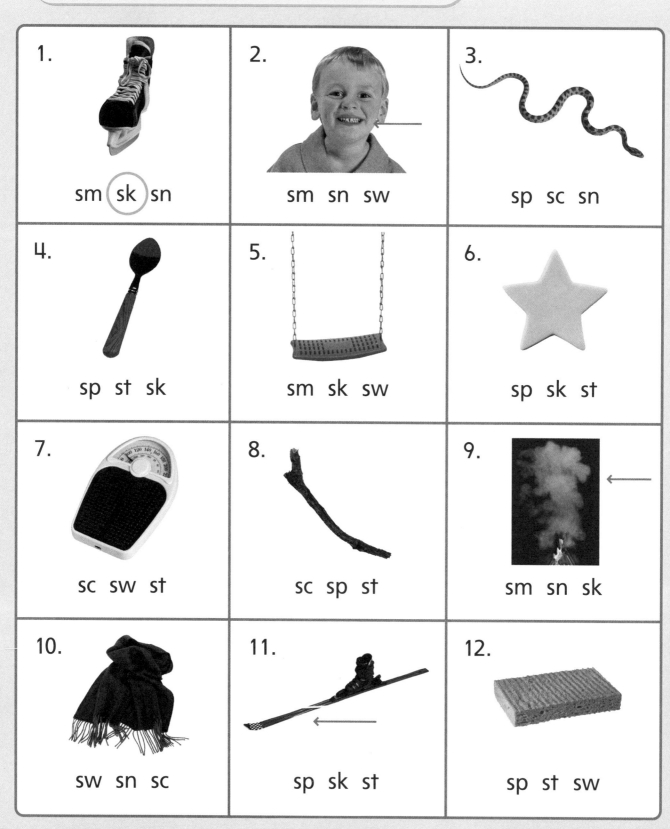

1. sm (sk) sn

2. sm   sn   sw

3. sp   sc   sn

4. sp   st   sk

5. sm   sk   sw

6. sp   sk   st

7. sc   sw   st

8. sc   sp   st

9. sm   sn   sk

10. sw   sn   sc

11. sp   sk   st

12. sp   st   sw

Name _____

Writing Initial Consonant Blends with *s*

 Say each picture's name. Write the letters that make the sounds at the beginning of the word. Read the words.

| sc | sk | sm | sn | sp | st | sw |

1.
____ im

2.
____ amp

3.
____ unk

 Listen to these clues. Write the missing letters. Read the words.

1. Another word for talk ____ eak

2. Not big ____ all

3. A three-legged seat ____ ool

4. A good taste ____ eet

5. Something to eat ____ ack

6. Another word for frightened ____ ared

Three-Letter Blends: *scr-, spr-, spl-, squ-, str-*

> Draw a line to connect the two pictures that begin with the same sound.

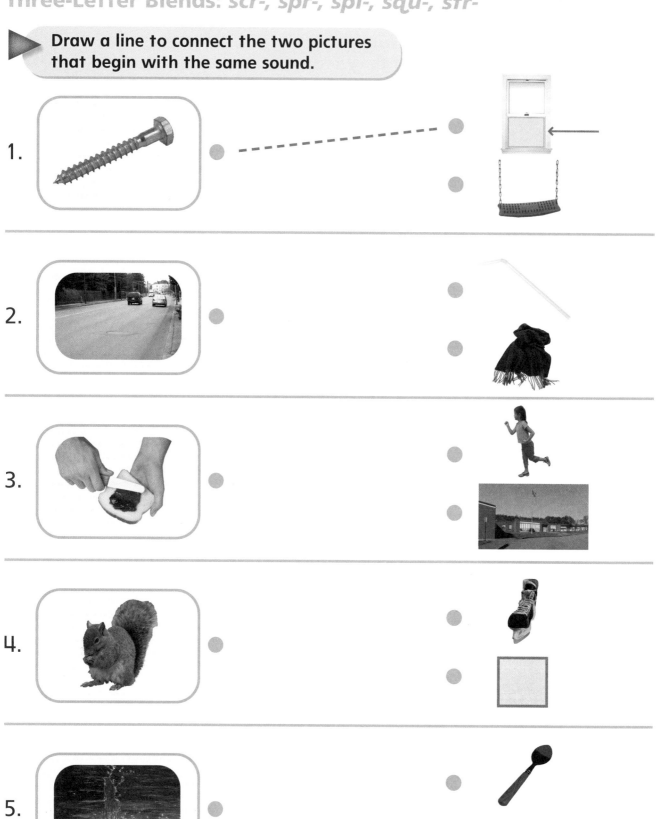

1.

2.

3.

4.

5.

Final Consonant Blends with *t: ct, ft, lt, nt, st*

 Say each picture's name. Write the missing letters. Read the words.

1.
_____
ra _____

2.
_____
te _____

3.
_____
toa _____

 Circle the word that completes the sentence. Write it on the line.

1. I _____ to go to the circus. (want) west

2. Ben stood in _____ of the class. frost   front

3. My dog Pal can _____ funny. ash   act

4. The bus _____ on time. left   last

5. Manny rode the little brown _____. colt   coat

Final Consonant Blends with *p* and *k*: *lk, mp, nk, rk, sk*

 Say each picture's name. Write the letters that make the sounds at the end of the word. Read the words.

1.	2.	3.	4.
la	mi	sha	bli

 Circle the word that completes the sentence. Write it on the line.

1. Diego and Tito went to _____. (camp) cake

2. The cat _____ all the milk. drove drank

3. I _____ I can run as fast as you. tramp think

4. A _____ is an animal with fur. mink mist

5. Pam will _____ to go to bed late. ask ant

Final Consonant Blends with *d: ld, nd, rd*

 Say each picture's name. Write the missing letters. Read the words.

1.	2. 	3. 	4. 
ha____	co____	ya____	sa____

 Circle the word that completes the sentence. Write it on the line.

1. Jack ran to the _____ of the lane. egg (end)

2. This rock is very _____ . hand hard

3. The _____ on this beach is hot. song sand

4. Lions and tigers are _____ animals. wind wild

5. I can _____ your hand. hold honk

Review Final Consonant Blends

Help Mike and Cate down the steps. Write the missing letters in the boxes. What is at the bottom of the steps?

| lift | tent | trunk | kind | dump | pump | pink |

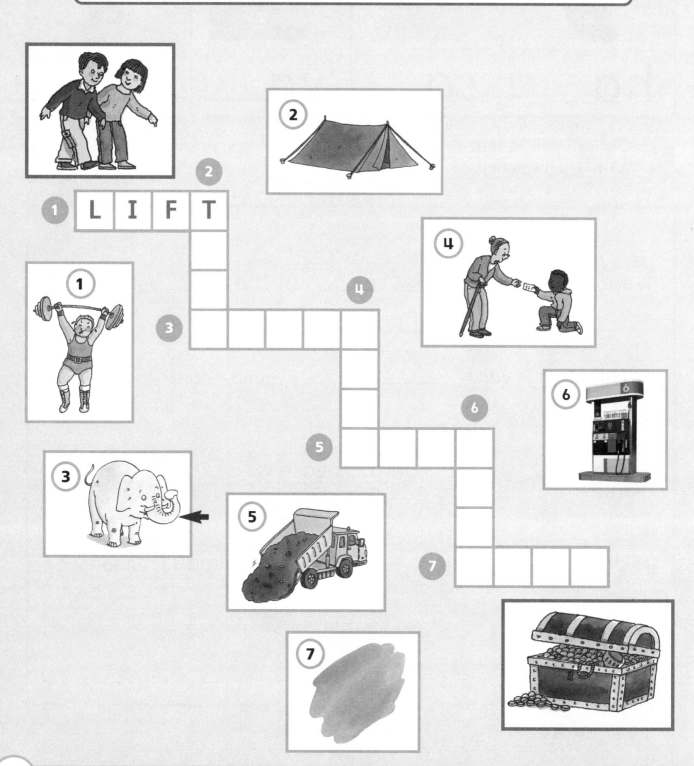

L I F T

Review Star Words

 Circle the Star Word in each sentence.

⭐ when   ⭐ there   ⭐ then   ⭐ where

(Where) is the popcorn?

There is the popcorn.

When can I get some?

At 6:00. You can get some then.

⭐ this   ⭐ those   ⭐ these   ⭐ that

Are those your pets?

No, these are my pets.

Is that your dog?

Yes, this is my dog.

Words with *-tch* and *-dge*

 Read the words in the box. Write each word under its picture.

badge	bridge	catch	watch	hedge	judge	match	pitch

1.

_____

2.

_____

3.

_____

4.

_____

5.

_____

6.

_____

7.

_____

8.

_____

Sentences with -*tch* and -*dge* Words

> **Read the sentence. Draw a line from each sentence to the picture that describes it. Underline all the -*dge* and -*tch* words in the sentences.**

1. Ava had a patch on her knee. ● ●

2. Dad baked a batch of cookies ● ●

3. Mitch went to the beach. ● ●

4. The box would not budge. ● ●

5. Midge went across the bridge. ● ●

6. The tree is on the edge of the cliff ● ●

7. Ben loves to eat fudge. ● ●

> Read these sentences with your child. Make up additional sentences using the underlined -*dge* and -*tch* words.

Read this poem. Talk about the questions.

Keep a poem in your pocket
and a picture in your head
and you'll never feel lonely
at night when you're in bed.

The little poem will sing to you
the little picture bring to you
a dozen dreams to dance to you
at night when you're in bed.

So-

Keep a picture in your pocket
and a poem in your head
and you'll never feel lonely
at night when you're in bed.

– Beatrice Schenk de Regniers

Think & Talk What does the poet mean when she says, "Keep a poem in your pocket?" How can a poem keep you from being lonely when you're in bed?

Write a Poem

 On the lines below, write your own poem. Remember, your poem can rhyme, but it does not have to.

Write about your feelings.	Write about your family.	Write about your favorite food.
Write about your pet.	Write about a color.	Write about a dream.

Parent Letter

Dear Parents,

As your child moves through second grade, you've probably noticed that he or she is becoming a more independent person. Your child is becoming a more independent reader and writer, too. Even though they are learning to do more and more on their own, children still need help to support and extend classroom learning.

What can you do at home to support your second grader's learning? Keep doing the Phonics Plus exercises marked with this icon 📖 . You can also:

- *Keep reading to your child*. In school, your child will probably read short books with chapters. You can read chapter books at home as well. Old favorites like *Charlotte's Web* by E. B. White and Laura Ingalls Wilder's *Little House on the Prairie* series will always make your nightly reading end with "To be continued . . ."

- *Look for language*. Children enjoy big words such as *Mississippi, hippopotamus,* and *supercalafragilisticexpialidocious*. Call attention to big words on billboards and signs and help your child sound them out.

- *Discover new books*. Go to the library and find out what's new. You'll be amazed at the number of new books arriving at the library. Many books written for younger children will make you and your second grader laugh. Don't overlook informational books on football, ballet, gerbils, and other things that interest your child.

- *Encourage writing*. In second grade, there is usually a heavy emphasis on writing. Read the stories, poems, and reports that your child brings home. Encourage your child to keep a diary, write a journal of a family trip, write notes to a sibling, or any other writing activity. Don't worry if the spelling is not perfect! As a writer, your child is a "work in progress."

Finally, remember that your child's learning continues after he or she leaves the classroom at the end of the day. What happens at home is powerful in helping your child learn to read and write.

Sincerely,

John F. Savage

Carta a los Padres

Queridos padres:

Es probable que haya notado que su hijo/hija se está convirtiendo en una persona más independiente. Pues también está empezando a leer y a escribir de una manera más independiente. Aunque esté aprendiendo más cosas y lo esté haciendo en solitario, su ayuda y su apoyo siguen siendo necesarios para ampliar los conocimientos adquiridos en el salón de clases.

¿Qué puede hacer usted desde casa para apoyar el aprendizaje de su hijo/hija durante el segundo grado? Sigan realizando los ejercicios de Phonics Plus indicados con este símbolo 📖. Otras formas de ayudar son:

- *Leyendo a su hijo/hija.* En la escuela seguramente estará leyendo relatos cortos con capítulos. Pues en casa también pueden leer libros con capítulos. Clásicos como *Las Telarañas de Carlota* de E. B. White y la serie *La casa de la pradera* de Laura Ingalls Wilder siempre le permitirán acabar su tiempo de lectura antes de dormirse con un "Continuará . . ."

- *Buscando palabras.* A los niños les divierten palabras como *Mesopotamia*, *hipopótamo* y *supercalifragilisticoespialidoso*. Llame la atención de su hijo/hija hacia palabras largas que aparecen en anuncios y en letreros, y ayúdele a pronunciarlas.

- *Descubriendo libros nuevos.* Vayan a la biblioteca y repasen los nuevos títulos. Le sorprenderá el número de libros nuevos que llegan a la biblioteca. Muchos libros escritos para niños más jóvenes provocarán su risa y la de su hijo/hija que ahora está en el segundo grado. No pasen por alto los libros informativos sobre fútbol, ballet, hámsters y otros temas que le interesen.

- *Animándole a escribir.* En el segundo grado se hace mucho hincapié en la escritura. Lea los cuentos, poemas y reportes que su hijo/hija traiga a casa. Anímele a llevar un diario, escribir un resumen de un viaje que hicieron en familia, escribir notas a un hermano o hermana, o cualquier otra actividad que conlleve la escritura. No se preocupe si comete errores de ortografía. Como escritor/escritora, el progreso de su hijo/hija está "en curso".

Por último, recuerde que el aprendizaje de su hijo/hija continúa al abandonar el salón de clases al final del día. Lo que ocurre en casa influye poderosamente en el desarrollo de sus habilidades lectoras y escritoras.

Atentamente,

John F. Savage

Why Monkeys Live in Trees

 Mike and Cate like this story about monkeys. Read it. Talk about the question.

Long ago, when the world was new, Lion was the king of all the animals.

"I am the king of the jungle," said Lion.

Lion and Monkey were good friends.

"I am your friend," said Monkey.

"And I am your friend," said Lion, "but I am still king of the jungle."

One night, when Lion was asleep, Monkey tied Lion's tail to a tree. When Lion woke up, he could not move. "Who tied my tail to a tree?" he growled.

Lion was angry. He roared. Monkey laughed. Lion roared some more. Monkey laughed some more. The more Lion roared, the more Monkey laughed.

At last, Tiger untied Lion's tail. Lion ran after Monkey. Monkey ran up a tree.

"Come down from there," Lion roared. But Monkey stayed right where he was. And that's where Monkey has lived ever since.

Think & Talk Why do you think Monkey tied Lion's tail to the tree?

Write a Story

 Write a story. Explain something in nature. Write some notes like the sample below. Then write your story on a separate sheet of paper.

This story is about: Why monkeys live in trees

The characters are: Lion, Monkey, Tiger

The setting is: the jungle

The problem is: Monkey needs to get away from Lion

The solution is: Monkey climbs a tree and lives there

My story is about:
_____
- -
_____

My characters are:
_____
- -
_____

My setting is:
_____
- -
_____

My problem is:
_____
- -
_____

My solution is:
_____
- -
_____

Short *a* Word Families

▶ Write consonants, blends, and digraphs on the lines to make words.

-ack	-ank	-ash
____ack	____ank	____ash
____ack	____ank	____ash
____ack	____ank	____ash

▶ Write three sentences using some of your words.

1. _____

2. _____

3. _____

Short *i* Word Families

 Write consonants, blends, and digraphs on the lines to make words.

-ick	-im	-ing
_____ ick	_____ im	_____ ing
_____ ick	_____ im	_____ ing
_____ ick	_____ im	_____ ing
_____ ick	_____ im	_____ ing
_____ ick	_____ im	_____ ing

 In each box, read the words. Connect the four words that rhyme. What shapes did you draw?

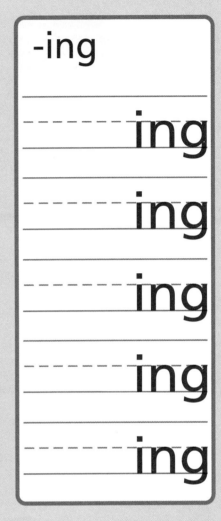

ball	bill	bell
bull	bin	bat
fill	still	spill

print	tint	mint
hop	hope	hill
hunt	hint	hot

dash	dish	drink
drip	dime	wash
fish	swish	wish

Short *u* Word Families

Write consonants, blends, and digraphs on the lines to make words.

-ump	-ush	-unk
___ ump	___ ush	___ unk
___ ump	___ ush	___ unk
___ ump	___ ush	___ unk
___ ump	___ ush	___ unk

 Write captions for these pictures.

1.

_____
_____

2.
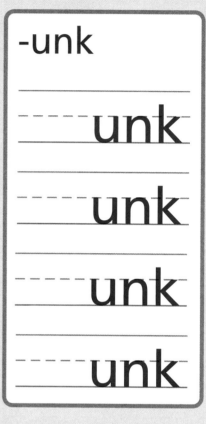
_____
_____

Name _____

Short o Word Families

 Write consonants, blends, and digraphs on the lines to make words.

-ock	-og	-op
_____ ock	_____ og	_____ op
_____ ock	_____ og	_____ op
_____ ock	_____ og	_____ op
_____ ock	_____ og	_____ op
_____ ock	_____ og	_____ op

 Play Rhyme Tic Tack Toe. In each box, circle three words in a row that rhyme.

shop	chop	shot
sod	not	sad
spot	sob	shock

job	block	rod
pond	frog	cot
shot	hot	knot

box	bog	mop
nod	fox	hop
pot	clock	shop

Short e Word Families

 Write consonants, blends, and digraphs
on the lines to make words.

-ell	-elt	-eck
___ell	___elt	___eck
___ell	___elt	___eck
___ell	___elt	___eck
___ell	___elt	___eck
___ell	___elt	___eck

 Unscramble these short e words. Write the words
on the lines. Read the words you make.

1. teg _____

2. ebd _____

3. sedk _____

4. lleps _____

5. htme _____

6. mne _____

Review Short Vowel Words

 Say the first picture's name. Change the vowel.
Write the new vowel and read the new word.

1.

cat   →   c __ t

2.

leg   →   l __ g

3.

dog   →   d __ g

4.

bug   →   b __ g

Read the Star Words in each box. Circle the Star Word that is used twice. Write that word on the line.

who **why** **how** **because**

1.

who   who   why

_____

- - - - - - - - - - - -

_____

2.

who   why   why

_____

- - - - - - - - - - - -

_____

3.

how   who   how

_____

- - - - - - - - - - - -

_____

4.

because because became

_____

- - - - - - - - - - - -

_____

 In each box, circle the three Star Words in a row that are the same.

who	how	why
where	who	when
how	what	who

hot	how	who
why	how	hat
who	how	hit

when	this	how
that	who	where
why	why	why

Name _____

Star Words: *who, why, how, because*

Read the Star Words. Write the best one in each sentence.

⭐ **who** ⭐ **why** ⭐ **how** ⭐ **because**

1. Jill knows ——————————— to play the trumpet.

2. Birds can fly ——————————— they have wings.

3. ——————————— do clouds float in the sky?

4. ——————————— is the coach of your team?

5. Tad knows ——————————— has the red cap.

6. You are my friend ——————————— I like you.

7. I wonder ——————————— the sky is blue.

8. ——————————— big is the sun?

Syllables

▶ How many syllables are in each animal's name? Write the answers in the circles.

elephants	giraffes
horses	monkeys
lions	zebras
tigers	dogs
camels	

Help your child write the animals' names in alphabetical order.

CVC Syllables

▶ **Read the words in the box. Write the best word in each sentence.**

bas•ket gar•den mit•ten blan•ket pic•nic sis•ter win•ter

1. Tam is Lee's _____.

2. Tam and Lee went on a _____.

3. They took a _____.

4. They rode their bikes to a _____

5. They put a _____ on the ground
   and then sat down.

6. They found an old _____ under
   a bush.

7. Tam had lost it last _____!

Have your child read the sentences on this page to you.
Talk about what might happen next to Tam and Lee.

Compound Words with CVC Parts

 Read the words in each box. Draw a line between the two words that will make a compound word. Write the word on the line.

1.
bath ●   ● pot

sink ●   ● tub

_____
- - - - - - - - - - - - - - - - - - - -
_____

2.
cab ●   ● cash

cat ●   ● fish

_____
- - - - - - - - - - - - - - - - - - - -
_____

3.
to ●   ● set

up ●   ● sit

_____
- - - - - - - - - - - - - - - - - - - -
_____

4.
egg ●   ● shell

bet ●   ● send

_____
- - - - - - - - - - - - - - - - - - - -
_____

5.
wink ●   ● mill

wind ●   ● milk

_____
- - - - - - - - - - - - - - - - - - - -
_____

6.
sun ●   ● sell

sad ●   ● set

_____
- - - - - - - - - - - - - - - - - - - -
_____

 Help your child use the compound words in this exercise in sentences.

Review Compound Words

 Circle all the compound words connected to *bathtub*. All the words go from left to right.

BEDBUG	**CATFISH**	**EGGSHELL**	**FOOTBALL**
SUNSET	**OUTSIDE**	**CLUBHOUSE**	

C	I	H	P	V	B	E	D	B	U	G
J	D	N	H	C	A	T	F	I	S	H
U	N	F	O	O	T	B	A	L	L	T
X	E	G	G	S	H	E	L	L	Q	S
S	U	N	S	E	T	T	X	E	R	W
K	F	M	A	O	U	T	S	I	D	E
G	B	C	L	U	B	H	O	U	S	E

 Help your child create his or her own word find using other compound words that you brainstorm together.

Adding -s and -es to CVC Words

Reminder
Add -es to words that end
with s, ss, ch, sh, x and z.
Add -s to all other words.

1. bus _____

2. dog _____

3. duck _____

4. box _____

5. cent _____

6. desk _____

7. dress _____

8. hat _____

9. dish _____

64 Lesson 31a

Name _____

Adding *-ed* and *-ing* to CVC Words

 Reminder
Double the final consonant in CVC words before adding *-ed* or *-ing*.

▶ Add *-ed* or *-ing* to the green word.
Write the missing word on the line.

1. Nan is _____ the string. cut

2. Bill _____ Fred on the back. tag

3. The dog is _____ his tail. wag

4. The cat _____ under the tree. nap

5. Sal is _____ a new cap. get

6. Tim is _____ at his desk. sit

7. Nell _____ the little kitten. pat

8. The dog _____ for a bit of ham. beg

9. The apple _____ in the sun. rot

10. Al said that he was _____ the contest. win

Short Vowel Base Words

 Read the sentences. Write the base word for the red word in each sentence.

1. _____ Tad mixes the sand.

2. _____ Nick is running fast.

3. _____ Jin packs her bag.

4. _____ Bill helped his sister.

5. _____ Jack has ten pets.

6. _____ Fran hopped up the step.

7. _____ Ben rushes to the store.

Name _____

Review Adding -s, -es, -ed, and -ing to Short Vowel Words

 Add endings to the base word. Write the new words. Read the new words.

1.

plan

s _____

ed _____

ing _____

2.

clap

s _____

ed _____

ing _____

3.

stop

s _____

ed _____

ing _____

4.

grin

s _____

ed _____

ing _____

 Read the words in the box. Write the best word in each sentence.

run ➡ ran   sit ➡ sat   hit ➡ hit

1. Yesterday, I _____ at my desk.

2. Yesterday, I _____ to the shop.

3. Yesterday, I _____ my hand on my bed.

Contractions with *am*, *is*, and *are*

 Read the words. Read the contractions. Draw lines to connect the words with their contraction.

1.

he is ●	● I'm
I am ●	● he's
that is ●	● we're
we are ●	● that's

2.

it is ●	● they're
she is ●	● she's
they are ●	● it's

 Make contractions with the red words. Write the contractions on the lines. Read the sentences.

1. That is _____ a big dog.

2. It is _____ six o'clock.

3. I am _____ happy.

4. We are _____ going to the circus.

5. They are _____ going to the circus with us.

6. She is _____ my sister.

7. He is _____ seven years old.

Name _____

Contractions with *will*, *have*, and *not*

 Read the words. Read the contractions. Draw lines to connect the words with their contraction.

1.		2.		3.	
he will •	• I'll	do not •	• don't	we have •	• I've
I will •	• you'll	will not •	• isn't	they have •	• you've
we will •	• he'll	is not •	• won't	you have •	• we've
you will •	• we'll	did not •	• didn't	I have •	• they've

 Make contractions with the red words. Write the contractions on the lines. Read the sentences.

1. I have _____ lost my cap.

2. It is _____ red and black.

3. I am _____ very sad.

4. I have _____ got good pals.

5. They will _____ help me look for it.

6. We will _____ find it soon.

Long *a* Word Families

 Write consonants, blends, and digraphs on the lines to make words.

-ate	-ake	-ane
_____ ate	_____ ake	_____ ane
_____ ate	_____ ake	_____ ane
_____ ate	_____ ake	_____ ane
_____ ate	_____ ake	_____ ane
_____ ate	_____ ake	_____ ane

 Read the words at the end of each sentence. Write the best word on each line.

1. My sister _____ to the _____.   came
                                                       game

2. Dave and I have the _____ _____.   same
                                                         name

3. We are _____ for the _____.   plane
                                                    late

Long *i* Word Families

 Write consonants, blends, and digraphs on the lines to make words.

-ide	-ine	-ice
_____ ide	_____ ine	_____ ice
_____ ide	_____ ine	_____ ice
_____ ide	_____ ine	_____ ice
_____ ide	_____ ine	_____ ice

 Read the questions. Draw a line from the question to the picture that answers it.

1. What tells time?   ●   ●

2. What is the same as a dime?   ●   ●

3. What do I ride?   ●   ●

4. What would you like to bite?   ●   ●

Long *u* Word Families

> In each box, circle the letter or letters that make a word.
> Write the letters on the line. Read the words.

1.

(c) f   s

_____
ube

2.

cr   ft   fl

_____
ute

3.

l   m   n

_____
ule

4.

bl   fl   t

_____
une

5.

s   d   t

_____
ube

6.

gl   pl   st

_____
ue

> Read each question. Circle *yes*
> or *no* to answer each question.

7. Can you play a tune on the flute?	yes	no
8. Is it bad to be rude?	yes	no
9. Does a cube have six sides?	yes	no
10. Is there sand on a dune?	yes	no
11. Does the sun shine in June?	yes	no
12. Can you make a rule?	yes	no

Long o Word Families

 Write consonants, blends, and digraphs on the lines to make words.

-ope	-ove	-one
___ ope	___ ove	___ one
___ ope	___ ove	___ one
___ ope	___ ove	___ one
___ ope	___ ove	___ one
___ ope	___ ove	___ one

 Read the words at the end of each sentence. Write the best word on each line.

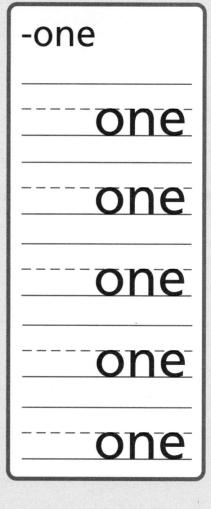

1. Tom has a red _____ at _____.   robe home

2. I _____ a _____ to Mona.   note wrote

3. Joan _____ her car into a _____.   hole drove

Review Long Vowel Words

1.	2.	3.
4.	5.	6.
7.	8.	9.

Read the words and definitions. Draw a line from each word to its definition.

1. eve   ●   ● the topic of a story

2. scheme ●   ● a plan

3. theme ●   ● the day before a holiday

Contractions with *will*, *is*, and *not*

Read the words. Read the contractions. Draw lines to connect the words with their contraction.

1.

she will ●---------● what's
they will ● ---● she'll
what is ● ● let's
let us ● ● they'll

2.

have not ● ● can't
can not ● ● aren't
are not ● ● haven't
does not ● ● doesn't

Read each sentence. Write the two words that make each contraction.

1. The sun doesn't shine at night. _____ _____

2. She'll hike up the hill. _____ _____

3. I can't ride my bike. _____ _____

4. They aren't at the game. _____ _____

5. What's the name of that snake? _____ _____

6. Let's go to the park. _____ _____

Compound Words with CVCe Parts

 Read the words in each box. Draw a line between the two words that make a compound word. Write the word on the line.

1.
bath ●   ● rode

sink ●   ● robe

_____

- - - - - - - - - - - - - - - - - - - -

_____

2.
pin ●   ● cake

pan ●   ● cube

_____

- - - - - - - - - - - - - - - - - - - -

_____

3.
out ●   ● side

to ●   ● sake

_____

- - - - - - - - - - - - - - - - - - - -

_____

4.
bad ●   ● time

bed ●   ● tide

_____

- - - - - - - - - - - - - - - - - - - -

_____

5.
shine ●   ● shop

space ●   ● ship

_____

- - - - - - - - - - - - - - - - - - - -

_____

6.
sun ●   ● smile

set ●   ● shine

_____

- - - - - - - - - - - - - - - - - - - -

_____

 Invent compound words with your child. Suggest words such as penphone, a pen that can also function as a telephone.

Syllables in CVCe Words

 Circle the CVCe syllable in each word. Write the best word in each sentence. Read the sentences.

| com•bine | com•plete | cos•tume | ex•plore |
| ig•nore | In•clude | in•vite | mis•take |

1. Bruce didn't make a _____.

2. Can you _____ the red blocks and the black blocks?

3. Ruth wore a cute _____.

4. Do not _____ the rules.

5. I hope you will _____ me to the game.

6. The kids will _____ the side of the hill.

7. Sal did the _____ job by himself.

8. _____ all the kids in your plans.

Adding -s to CVCe words

Read each picture's name. Write the plural form on the line.

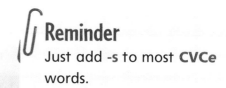
Reminder
Just add -s to most **CVCe** words.

1. slide   _____

2. smile   _____

3. rose   _____

4. cake   _____

5. mule   _____

Reminder
If a **CVCe** word ends with -fe, change the **f** to **v** and add -s.

6. knife   _____

7. wife   _____

Make a list of common household objects. Have your child give you the plural form of each word on the list.

Adding *-ed* and *-ing* to CVCe Words

 Add *-ed* or *-ing*. Write the missing word in the sentence. Read the sentences.

trade + ed = traded	trade + ing = trading

_____
- - - - - - - - - -
ride   1. Mike was _____ his bike too fast.

_____
- - - - - - - - - -
come
take   2. He was _____ to a corner and was

_____
- - - - - - - - - -
_____ a turn.

_____
- - - - - - - - - -
scrape   3. Mike fell off his bike and _____ his leg.

_____
- - - - - - - - - -
4. His mother _____ the scrape on his leg.

tape   5. "Next time you should be more careful

ride
_____
- - - - - - - - - -
_____ your bike," she told Mike.

CVC and CVCe Base Words

 Read the sentences. Write the base word for the red word on the line.

1. _____ Mike was mopping the floor.

2. _____ Luke was hoping for a prize.

3. _____ The dog begged for a bone.

4. _____ The kangaroo hopped up the steps.

5. _____ The sun was shining.

6. _____ Sam is baking a cake.

7. _____ The cat napped under a tree.

8. _____ Ben hugged his pet.

9. _____ The snake was hiding in the bush.

10. _____ The kids were sliding down the hill.

Review Adding -s, -ed, and -ing to CVCe Words

▶ **Add endings to the base word. Write the new words. Read the new words.**

1. **smile**
s _____
ed _____
ing _____

2. **hope**
s _____
ed _____
ing _____

3. **trade**
s _____
ed _____
ing _____

4. **slope**
s _____
ed _____
ing _____

5. **skate**
s _____
ed _____
ing _____

6. **price**
s _____
ed _____
ing _____

7. **race**
s _____
ed _____
ing _____

8. **close**
s _____
ed _____
ing _____

CV Words

▶ **Read the words in the box. Write the best word in each sentence.**

be	he	she	me	we	No	so	go

_____

1. My dad gave _____ ten cents.

_____

2. Pam said that _____ are going to the circus.

_____

3. Will you _____ my pal?

_____

4. I'm tired, _____ I'm going to bed.

_____

5. _____ , I won't sit there.

_____   _____

6. Jack said that _____ would _____ up the hill.

_____

7. Jill said that _____ wouldn't.

Open Syllables

 Say each picture's name. Spell the word on the lines.
Write one letter on each line. Read the words.

1.

____ ____ ____ ____ ____

- - - - - ● - - - - - -

____ ____ ____ ____

2.

____ ____ ____ ____ ____ ____

- - - - - ● - - - - - -

____ ____ ____ ____ ____ ____

3.

____ ____ ____ ____

- - - - ● - - - - -

____ ____ ____ ____

4.

____ ____ ____ ____

- - - - - - ● - - - - - - -

____ ____ ____ ____

 Read the words in the box. Write
the best word in each sentence.

| fever   later   minus   moment   music |

_____

- - - - - - - - -

5. Sal is sick. He has a _____.

_____

- - - - - - - -

6. The flute makes nice _____.

_____

- - - - - - - - -

7. Ten _____ seven is three.

_____

- - - - - - - - -

8. A _____ is only a short time.

_____

- - - - - - - - -

9. We'll go to lunch _____.

Three Kinds of Open Syllables

 Read the words in the box. Sort them by syllable pattern. Write the words on the lines.

e•ven e•vil ha•lo hu•man
mu•sic o•ver po•lo re•cent
si•lent su•per u•nit

o•pen

_____
- - - - - - - - - - - - - - - - -
_____
- - - - - - - - - - - - - - - - -
_____
_____
- - - - - - - - - - - - - - - - -
_____

so•lo

_____
- - - - - - - - - - - - - - - - -
_____
- - - - - - - - - - - - - - - - -
_____

pa•per

_____
_____
- - - - - - - - - - - - - - - - -
_____
_____
- - - - - - - - - - - - - - - - -
_____
_____
- - - - - - - - - - - - - - - - -
_____

Write a sentence that uses one word from each box above.

- -
_____
- -

y as a Vowel

> Say each picture's name. If the *y* has a long *e* sound, circle the letter *e*. If the *y* has a long *i* sound, circle *i*.

1.
   e ⓘ

2.
   e   i

3.
   e   i

4.
   e   i

5.
   e   i

6.
   e   i

7.
   e   i

8.
   e   i

9.
   e   i

10.
    e   i

11.
    e   i

12.
    e   i

Read the words in the box. Sort the words by sound. Write the words on the lines.

body   dry   happy   monkey   my   sky

fly
_____
_____
_____
_____

baby
_____
_____
_____
_____

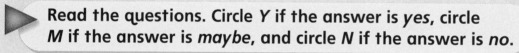 **Read the questions. Circle *Y* if the answer is *yes*, circle *M* if the answer is *maybe*, and circle *N* if the answer is *no*.**

1. Can I fly into the sky?   Y   M   N

2. Does candy make me happy?   Y   M   N

3. Does a fox try to be sly?   Y   M   N

4. Is a puppy as tiny as a bunny?   Y   M   N

5. Is a baby happy when he's sleepy? Y   M   N

6. Can a monkey have money?   Y   M   N

Name _____

Adding -es and -ed to Words with *y*

Reminder

Before you add -es or -ed to words that end in y, change the y to i.

 Add -es to the green words. Write the words on the lines.

fly _____   pony _____

\- - - - - - - - - -   \- - - - - - - - - -

1. Brush the _____ off the _____.

story _____

\- - - - - - - - - -

2. The teacher told us two _____.

cry _____   try _____

\- - - - - - - - - -   \- - - - - - - - - -

3. My baby sister _____ when he _____ to pick her up.

bunny _____

\- - - - - - - - - -

4. Cute _____ hide behind the fence.

 Add -ed to the green words. Write the words on the lines.

tidy _____

\- - - - - - - - - -

5. We _____ our desks before going home.

fry _____

\- - - - - - - - - -

6. I like _____ eggs and ham.

pry _____

\- - - - - - - - - -

7. Tommy _____ the lid off the jar.

Adding -ly

Read the words in each box. Draw a line from the base word to the -ly word.

1.			2.		
safe ●		● nicely	shy ●		● wisely
nice ●		● sadly	wise ●		● shyly
brave ●		● safely	blind ●		● silently
sad ●		● bravely	silent ●		● blindly

Write the -ly form of the green word. Read the sentences.

1. The puppy ran ＿＿＿＿＿ away from the cat. quick

2. The man spoke ＿＿＿＿＿ to the kids. soft

4. The river runs ＿＿＿＿＿ down the hill. swift

5. We will ＿＿＿＿＿ help you clean the place. glad

6. The sun sets ＿＿＿＿＿ at dusk. slow

Dictate a list of adjectives to your child. Have him or her add -ly to the word and use it in a sentence.

Base Words with *y*

Bobby and Suzy are friends with Mike and Cate. Read about their party. Write the base word for each red word on the lines. Talk about the question.

The Costume Party

Bobby and Suzy went to a costume party. They dressed like (1) bunnies. Their baby sisters dressed like (2) puppies. They played games and (3) tried to win (4) pennies for a prize. They rode (5) ponies. Two (6) ladies told (7) stories. They had cake and (8) candies. They had a (9) lovely time. They (10) tidied up after the party.

"I love (11) parties," said Bobby.

"So do I, "said Suzy. "I would (12) gladly go to parties any time."

1. _____

2. _____

3. _____

4. _____

5. _____

6. _____

7. _____

8. _____

9. _____

10. _____

11. _____

12. _____

 What makes costume parties fun?

Stress

 Read the words in the box. If the stress is on the first syllable, write the word in the first column. If the stress is on the second syllable, write the word in the second column.

awake	baby	behind	candy	center
finish	himself	raccoon	sister	today

1

_____

_____

_____

_____

_____

_____

2

_____

_____

_____

_____

_____

_____

 Help your child write each column of words in alphabetical order. Have your child read the words to you, exaggerating the accented syllable.

90   Lesson 44a

Schwa

 Read the words in each box. Draw a line connecting each word with its phonetic spelling

basket ● - - - - - - - ● mag' nət

cabin ●   ● ca' bən

magnet ●   ● bas' kət

pencil ●   ● ə wōk'

ticket ●   ● tik' ət

awoke ●   ● pen' səl

cancel ●   ● hon' əst

distant ●   ● can' səl

honest ●   ● dis' tənt

 Look up words you know in the dictionary. Write four words with the schwa sound.

1. _____   2. _____

3. _____   4. _____

 Help your child use the four words he or she chose at the bottom of the page in sentences.

Star Words: *always, never, before, after*

 Circle the Star Word that is used twice in each box. Write that word on the line.

always **never** **before** **after**

1.

| **always** **after** **always** |

_____

- - - - - - - - - - - - - - - - -

_____

2.

| **before** **never** **never** |

_____

- - - - - - - - - - - - - - - - -

_____

3.

| **before** **before** **always** |

_____

- - - - - - - - - - - - - - - - -

_____

4.

| **after** **always** **after** |

_____

- - - - - - - - - - - - - - - - -

_____

Write the best Star Word from above in each sentence.

_____

- - - - - - - - - - -

5. The sun _____ rises in the east.

_____

- - - - - - - - - - -

6. June comes _____ May.

_____

- - - - - - - - - - -

7. I wash my face _____ I go to bed.

_____

- - - - - - - - - - -

8. You should _____ touch a hot stove.

Name _____

Star Words: *always, never, before, after*

 Count the Star Words in the box. Write the number of times you see each word on the line.

1. after _____

2. always _____

3. because _____

4. before _____

5. how _____

6. never _____

7. who _____

8. why _____

because

why   who

always

why   never

HOW   who

before

how   why

after

before

because

who   always

Read the words in the box. Sort the words by sound. Write the words on the lines.

chart	crate	champ	fan	fade	far	lake	large
lack	shake	shack	shark	star	stack	stake	

car

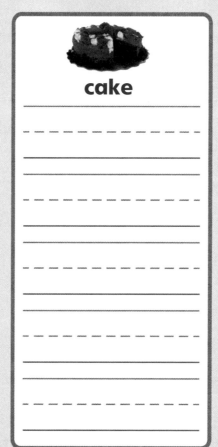

cake

cat

 Read each set of words. Draw a line to connect the words with the picture that describes them.

1. a large jar

2. a dark cart

3. a smart shark

4. a star on a barn

Words with -or

 Read the words in the box. Sort the words by sound. Write the words on the lines.

| born bone bog home horse hot note not |
| north spot sport spoke storm stone stop |

corn

_____

cone

_____

cot

_____

 Read each set of words. Draw a line to connect the words with the picture that describes them.

1. a horse on a porch

2. a lord in a fort

3. a fork in a horn

4. a stork in a storm

Words with *-er, -ir,* and *-ur*

Read the words in each box. Write the best word on the lines. Read the sentences.

---

chirped	bird	perched

_____

Dirk saw a _____ in the sky. The bird

_____

_____ on a branch and _____ a song.

---

skirt	twirled	first

_____

Marcy marched _____ .

_____

She wore a red _____ and she _____ a
baton.

---

turtle	girl	ferns	hurt	nurse

_____   _____

A _____ is hiding in the _____ .

_____   _____

The turtle is _____ . The _____

_____

will save it and bring it to the _____ .

---

96   Lesson 47a

r-Controlled Vowels in Compound Words

▶ **Read the words in each box. Draw a line between the two words that will make a compound word. Write the word on the line.**

1. star ● ----- ● rock
short ● ----- ● fish
_____
- - - - - - - - - - - - - -
_____

2. bark ●   ● yard
back ●   ● yell
_____
- - - - - - - - - - - - - -
_____

3. fire ●   ● works
fine ●   ● wakes
_____
- - - - - - - - - - - - - -
_____

4. birds ●   ● try
birth ●   ● day
_____
- - - - - - - - - - - - - -
_____

▶ **Read the words in the box. Circle the syllable with the *r*-controlled vowel in each word. Write the best word in each sentence.**

artist   orbits   market

_____
- - - - - - - - - - -
5. We will buy some fruit at the _____.

_____
- - - - - - - - - - -
6. Marcy wants to be an _____.

_____
- - - - - - - - - - -
7. The earth _____ around the sun.

Popcorn

 Mike and Cate love popcorn. Read to learn where popcorn comes from. Talk about the question.

Most kids love popcorn. But where does popcorn come from? Popcorn comes from corn that grows on farms. It is a special kind of corn.

First, the farmer plants corn seeds. The corn seeds grow to tall corn plants.

Next, the farmer harvests the corn. The farmer takes the yellow kernels off the corn cob. The outside of the kernel becomes very hard. Inside each kernel is a tiny drop of water. When the kernel is heated, the water turns to steam. The middle of the kernel gets bigger and bigger.

Then **POP!** It explodes. The hard, yellow kernel turns into a fluffy, white snack.

Finally, we eat the popcorn. Yum, yum!

 What makes popcorn pop?

Popcorn: Sequencing

 Write *first, next, then,* or *finally* next to the correct picture.
Write a sentence that describes each picture.

first	next	then	finally

Fill in the blanks with *-all* words. Then write three sentences using some of these *-all* words.

ball

1. _____

2. _____

3. _____

Review Vowels

 Say each picture's name. Circle the word with the same vowel sound.

1.	2. 	3. 
wax (hall) whale	cake cab call	dart date dance

4. 	5. 	6. 
came call car	fall fast fake	ant all ate

7. 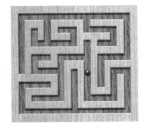	8. 	9. 
shack shade sharp	large lake land	tag tame tall

10. 	11. 	12. 
stall stack stage	fall flag flame	small smart snake

Review Word Patterns

Read the words in the box. Sort the words by spelling pattern. Write the words on the lines.

bad	be	black	far	flag	go	math	no	page
park	plate	serve	shade	she	storm	tape		

CVC	CVCe	CV	CV-r
cat	cake	me	car

Help your child make up sentences. Use one word from each column in each sentence.

Missing Word Parts

 Say each picture's name. Fill in the letters that complete each compound word. Read the words.

1.

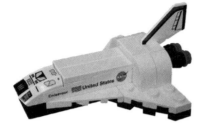

__ __ __ __ __ __

space__ __ __ __ __ __

2.

__ __ __ __ __

__ __ __ __ __ __ fish

3.

__ __ __ __ __ __ __

pop__ __ __ __ __ __

4.

__ __ __ __ __

__ __ __ __ __ __ mill

5.

__ __ __ __ __

back__ __ __ __ __ __

6.

__ __ __ __ __

__ __ __ __ __ cakes

 Dictate the words on this page to your child. Have him or her break the word into its two parts, then spell each part of the word.

Cate's favorite color is red. Read this poem about her favorite color. Talk about the question.

Red is a sunset
Blazy and bright
Red is feeling brave
With all your might.
Red is a sunburn
Spot on your nose,
Sometimes red
Is a red, red rose.
Red is a lipstick,
Red is a shout.
Red is a signal
That says: "Watch out!"
Red is a great big
Rubber ball
Red is the giant-est
Color of all.
Red is a show-off
No doubt about it.
But can you imagine
Living without it?
　　　　—Mary O'Neill

 What would life be like without the color red?

Figurative Language

What do these colors make you think of? Write what you think of on the lines. Add your own color for the last part.

What Is Red?

As red as _____

As red as _____

As red as _____

As red as _____

What Is Blue?

As blue as _____

As blue as _____

As blue as _____

As blue as _____

What Is Yellow?

As yellow as _____

As yellow as _____

As yellow as _____

As yellow as _____

What Is _____?

As _____ as _____

As _____ as _____

As _____ as _____

As _____ as _____

Talk about colors with your child. What is his or her favorite? What is your favorite? Why?

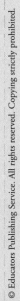

Parent Letter

Dear Parents,

As your child moves through second grade and gets better at reading, what you do at home remains very important. Keep doing the *Phonics Plus* exercises marked with this icon 📖. You should also keep on doing the other things you've been doing all along, including:

- *Never missing a chance to read with your child.* Set aside a time each evening. Turn off the TV and make family reading time. Visit your library and ask the librarian to recommend books. Don't forget informational books on knights, volcanoes, gerbils, dinosaurs, and other topics that your child is interested in. Have your child read to you the storybooks that he or she brings home from school.

- *Pointing out new words on trips to the supermarket and the mall.* Talk about the meaning of these words. Look for messages on signs and billboards as you drive around town. Print is all around you. Use this print to help your child learn to read. On longer trips in the car, play tapes of favorite stories that capture your child's interest.

- *Encouraging your child to write.* Have your child help you write the grocery list and reminder notes to put on the refrigerator. Put notes in your child's lunchbox like "Have fun in school today!" or "We are having your favorite dinner tonight!" When you run out of ideas, write jokes or riddles, the sillier the better. You can find lots of children's books of jokes and riddles at your local library or bookstore. Have your child add a note to your lunchbox. You can even encourage your child to write stories for you to read. Make a big deal out of what they write. Don't expect all the words to be spelled right. Correct spelling will come in time. The words and ideas your child uses are more important at this point.

All the help and support that you provide at home will pay off as your child grows in reading and writing.

Sincerely,

John F. Savage

Carta a los Padres

Queridos padres:

Mientras su hijo/hija progresa en el segundo grado y aprende a leer mejor, lo que hacen en casa sigue siendo muy importante. Sigan realizando los ejercicios de *Phonics Plus* indicados con este símbolo 📖. También deberían seguir realizando las otras actividades que han venido haciendo hasta ahora, como:

- *Aprovechando cualquier oportunidad para leer consu hijo/hija.* Reserven tiempo cada noche. Apaguen el televisor y lean en familia. Vayan a la biblioteca y pidan a un bibliotecario/bibliotecaria que les recomiende libros. No se olviden de los libros informativos sobre caballeros, volcanes, hámsters, dinosaurios y otros temas que le interesen a su hijo/hija. Haga que él o ella le lea los libros de cuentos que trae a casa de la escuela.

- *Señalando palabras nuevas cuando vayan al supermercado y al centro comercial.* Hablen del significado de estas palabras. Busquen mensajes en los letreros y anuncios mientras manejan por su pueblo o ciudad. Hay letras impresas por todas partes. Utilícelas para ayudar a su hijo/hija a leer. Cuando hagan viajes más largos, utilicen el tocacintas para escuchar los cuentos que captan su interés.

- *Animándo le a su hijo/hija a escribir.* Haga que su hijo/hija le escriba la lista de la compra y recordatorios para poner en la nevera. Déjele notas en la lonchera, como: "¡Pásalo bien en la escuela!" o "¡Esta noche cenamos tu plato favorito!" Cuando se le acaben las ideas, escriba chistes o adivinanzas, cuanto más tontas mejor. Podrá encontrar muchos libros de chistes y adivinanzas para niños en la biblioteca o en una librería. Haga que su hijo/hija le ponga una nota en su lonchera. Incluso le puede animar a escribir cuentos para que usted los lea. Celebre por todo lo alto sus logros como escritor. No espere que todas las palabras estén escritas correctamente. Aprenderá la ortografía a su debido tiempo. En este momento las palabras e ideas utilizadas son más importantes.

Toda la ayuda y el apoyo que le proporcione a su hijo/hija en casa merecerán la pena cuando compruebe cómo se desarrollan sus habilidades lectoras y escritoras.

Atentamente,

John F. Savage

Read this story. Talk about the question.

Long ago, in a village in the mountains, lived a man who hated night. During the day, he was happy working on his farm. He milked cows, fed chickens, and planted corn. All day long, he would smile and sing.

But when the sun went down and his world turned dark, he would become very sad.

"I don't like you," he would yell at the night.

One day, as the sun was setting, the man climbed to the top of the mountain.

"Stop," he said to the night. "Please don't come. When you come, my happiness goes away. What do you do with the sunlight that makes me so happy?"

Night answered, "I must come. I can't stop. The sunlight hides behind me." The man came down the mountain very sad. But he had an idea!

The next day, as the sun was setting, he climbed to the very top of the mountain. He stood on his tiptoes and poked a hole with his finger through the sky. A tiny ray of light shone through. Then he made another hole and another ray of light came through. He did it again and again all over the sky, and the dark sky was full of tiny spots of light.

The man was so happy he jumped up and raised his fist. His fist made a large hole.

And that's why the stars and moon are in the sky.

All the people in the village danced and sang because night was not so dark any more!

Why do you think ancient people made up stories like these about the world around them?

Word Families with *ai*

 Write consonants, blends, and digraphs on the lines to make words.

-ail	-ain	-ate
_____ail	_____ain	_____ate
_____ail	_____ain	_____ate
_____ail	_____ain	_____ate
_____ail	_____ain	_____ate
_____ail	_____ain	_____ate

 Read the words at the end of each sentence. Write the best word on each line.

1. The _____ got on the _____.   maid
train

2. The man will _____ for the _____.   mail
wait

3. This ship can _____ to _____.   Spain
sail

4. Gail put _____ into the _____.   pail
bait

5. The dog has a _____ _____.   plain
tail

Word Families with *oa*

Write consonants, blends, and digraphs
on the lines to make words.

-oat	-oad	-oal
____oat	____oad	____oal
____oat	____oad	____oal
____oat	____oad	____oal

Read the questions. Circle *yes* or *no*
to answer each question.

1. Can a coach roam at a game?   (yes)   no

2. Can a goat moan and groan?   yes   no

3. Can Joan wear a cloak at a party?   yes   no

4. Can a toad float in a lake?   yes   no

5. Can a man put a load of soap on a truck? yes   no

Alphabetical Order

 Read the words in each box. Write them on the lines in alphabetical order.

1.

| boat | aid | chain |

_____

_____

_____

2.

| hail | grain | fail |

_____

_____

_____

3.

| loan | nail | pail |
| oak | maid |

_____

_____

_____

_____

_____

4.

| quail | soak | roast |
| trail | pain |

_____

_____

_____

_____

_____

Choose the Correct Spelling

 Say each picture's name. Circle the correct spelling.

1.

(cage) caig

2.

nale   nail

3.

cake   caik

4.

rake   raik

5.

trane   train

6.

snale   snail

7.

tode   toad

8.

rope   roap

9.

toste   toast

10.

stone   stoan

11.

gote   goat

12.

bote   boat

Words with ee

 Say each picture's name. Circle the correct word for each picture.

1.  chimp (cheese) cheap	2. foot fret feet	3.  jeep jet jump
4.  snail snake sneeze	5.  truth teach teeth	6.  steel street sweet

 Say each picture's name. Write the word next to the picture.

7. _____	8. 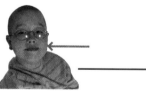 _____
9.  _____	10. _____
11. _____	12. _____

Name _____

Words with *ea*

▶ Say each picture's name. Circle the correct word for each picture.

1.  beach bread brief	2.  mail meat mean	3.  laugh lead leaf
4.  seal sold sail	5.  tame time team	6.  beds beads bread

▶ Read the words in the box. Write each picture's name underneath it.

peach   beak   seat   peas

7. _____	8.  _____
9. _____	10.  _____

The Soccer Game

The game was tied. The green team had three goals and we had three goals.

Pete Breen kicked the ball to me. It did not seem like a hard kick. The ball came to me but I did not see it. It hit my knee. I could see it go deep into the goal. We scored! We beat the green team, four to three.

My teammates ran to me. They screamed and cheered. I could not speak. It was like a dream. It was a sweet feeling.

 Why do some people get so excited at games?

Review Vowel Pairs

**Read the words in the box and find them in the puzzle.
All the words go left to right or top to bottom.**

beach	coat	chain	grain	nail	oats	queen
sneak	soap	sweet	stain	toast	wheel	treat

S	N	E	A	K	S	W	E	E	T
O	A	T	S	Y	T	H	I	Q	O
A	I	D	B	R	A	E	G	U	A
P	L	S	E	Z	I	E	R	E	S
T	R	E	A	T	N	L	A	E	T
A	N	D	C	O	A	T	I	N	N
O	F	C	H	A	I	N	N	O	T

Help your child give you definitions of each of the words in the word find. Take turns using these words in sentences.

Read the words. Add *-er* or *-est* to make new words. Write the new words.

	-er	-est
1. deep	_____	_____
2. green	_____	_____
3. sweet	_____	_____
4. weak	_____	_____
5. clean	_____	_____
6. neat	_____	_____

 Circle the tree that the sentence describes.

 This tree is tall.

 This tree is taller.

 This tree is tallest.

Inflectional Suffixes *-er* and *-est*

> **Read the sentences. Write the correct form of the red base word in each blank.**

1. The river is deep. The lake is _____.

   The sea is the _____ of all.

2. The cat is fast. The fox is _____.

   The cheetah is _____ of all.

3. A kitten is small. A chipmunk is _____.

   An ant is _____ of all.

4. The zebra is tall. The camel is _____.

   The giraffe is _____ of all.

 Reminder
What about **good** and **bad**?
We don't say **gooder** and
badder! We say:

| good | better | best |
| bad | worse | worst |

 With your child, compare things around the house. Which plant is greenest? Which room is biggest? Smallest? Loudest?

Adding -er and -est to CVC and CVCe Words

 Read the words. Add the endings -er and -est. Write the new words you make.

	-er	-est
1. big	_____	_____
2. brave	_____	_____
3. red	_____	_____
4. rude	_____	_____
5. wet	_____	_____
6. cute	_____	_____

 Circle the red word that describes the clock in each picture.

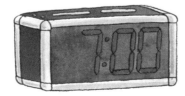 It is (late.)

 It is late / later.

 It is latest / later.

Base Words with *-er* and *-est*

 Read the sentences. Write the base word for the red word in each sentence.

1. Jane's dog is bigger than Tina's cat. _____

2. My dog was the cutest puppy. _____

3. A elephant is larger than a tiger. _____

4. Jack got the finest gifts for his birthday. _____

5. This banana is riper than that banana. _____

6. An inch is shorter than a foot. _____

7. The boy has the saddest look on his face. _____

 Circle the red word that describes each picture.

 It is (hot.)

 It is hotter / hot.

 It is hottest / hotter.

Vowel Digraph oo

Say each picture's name. Write the word under the picture. Read the words.

1.

_____

2.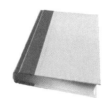

_____

3.

_____

4.

_____

5.

_____

6.

_____

7.

_____

8.

_____

9.

_____

10.

_____

11.

_____

12.

_____

Vowel Digraph *oo*

 Write consonants, blends, and digraphs on the lines to make words.

-oon	-ook
_____ oon	_____ ook
_____ oon	_____ ook
_____ oon	_____ ook
_____ oon	_____ ook
_____ oon	_____ ook

 Read the questions. Circle *Y* if the answer is yes, circle *M* if the answer is maybe, and circle *N* if the answer is no.

1. Does a horse have a hoof? Y M N

2. Is a goose covered with wool? Y M N

3. Are cookies good food? Y M N

4. Can a moose moo? Y M N

5. Can you shampoo a kangaroo? Y M N

6. Can a spoon be made of wood? Y M N

7. Can a crook steal a broom? Y M N

8. Is a balloon smooth? Y M N

Read this passage. Talk about the questions.

I can see the moon. It looks like a big balloon in the sky.

The surface of the moon is not smooth. It is covered with rocks and dirt. The moon has mountains. It has big holes called craters and dark, flat spaces too. You can see these spaces when you look at the moon.

The moon shines at night.

Sometimes the moon looks like this:

Sometimes it looks like this:

And sometimes it looks like this:

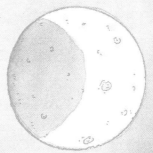

Some nights we cannot see the moon at all.

But the moon has no light of its own. It is made of rock. It reflects the light from the sun, just as a mirror reflects the light from a flashlight.

Spacemen have landed on the moon. They picked up rocks to bring back to earth. People study these rocks to learn what the moon is like.

 Why does the moon seem to change shape? How did scientists figure this out?

Name _____

Looking at the Moon: Assessment

 Fill in the bubble in front of the best answer for each question.

1. What is the moon made of?
   Ⓐ rock
   Ⓑ cheese
   Ⓒ light
   Ⓓ wood

2. Why did spacemen bring rocks back from the moon?
   Ⓐ to play with
   Ⓑ to study
   Ⓒ to build houses
   Ⓓ to plant

3. How does the moon give light?
   Ⓐ It shines all by itself.
   Ⓑ It reflects light from the earth.
   Ⓒ It reflects light from the sun.
   Ⓓ It has a fire inside of it.

4. Find the word that has the same sound as <u>dark</u>.
   Ⓐ damp
   Ⓑ bark
   Ⓒ work
   Ⓓ bare

5. Which word has been divided into syllables correctly?
   Ⓐ b•alloon
   Ⓑ bal•loon
   Ⓒ ballo•on
   Ⓓ balloo•n

6. The moon reflects the light from the sun, just as a mirror reflects the light from a flashlight. What does the word <u>reflect</u> mean in that sentence?
   Ⓐ give back
   Ⓑ reduce
   Ⓒ bright
   Ⓓ race

Read the words in the box. Write the best word in each sentence.

> **caught   fault   launch   lawn   paws   saw   straw   yawn**

1. The kids ran across the grass on the _____.

2. I fell off my bike, but it was not my _____.

3. Paul _____ his friend at the mall.

4. They will _____ the spaceship next week.

5. I like to drink milk through a _____.

6. My small puppy has big _____.

7. When I'm sleepy, I _____.

8. The dog jumped and _____ the ball.

 Have your child read the sentences on this page to you. Together, sort the words in the box by spelling pattern (*au* and *aw*).

Vowel Digraphs *au* and *aw*

 Read the words in the box. Sort them by spelling pattern. Write the words with *aw* under *claw*. Write the words with *au* under *cause*.

caught fault launch lawn paws saw laundry yawn

claw	cause
_____	_____
_____	_____
_____	_____
_____	_____

 Read the words in the box. Write each word next to its meaning.

August autumn sausage laundry hawk dawn

_____ 1. something to eat

_____ 2. a large bird

_____ 3. a season of the year

_____ 4. a month of the year

_____ 5. sunrise

_____ 6. what we wash

Vowel Digraph *ie*

> **Read the words. Draw a line to connect the words with the picture that describes them.**

1. two pennies ●   ●

2. three flies ●   ●

3. brown puppies ● ●

4. crying baby ●   ●

5. green field ●   ●

6. cherry pie ●   ●

> **Write the name of your best friend.**

Reminder
The word **friend** has the vowel pair ie, but it makes the **short e** sound as in Fred.

_____ is my best _____.

Vowel Digraph *ea*

Read the words. Draw a line to connect the words with the picture that describes them.

1. piece of steak   •   •

2. red leaf   •   •

3. green sweater   •   •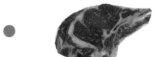

4. spool of thread   •   •

5. green peas   •   •

6. string of beads   •   •

Write a sentence using the words *great*, *break*, or *steak*.

Reminder
Words like **great** and **break** have the vowel pair **ea**, but it makes the **long a** sound in these words.

_____

Review Vowel Digraphs

Say each picture's name. Fill in *oo, au, aw, ie,* or *ea* to make a word. Read the words.

1
f___ther

2.
c___kies

3.
br___ m___

4.
fr___nds

5.
f___ld

6.
l___nch

7.
b___k

8.
racc___n

9.
br___d

10.
str___

11.
p___ch

12.
r___ster

Name _____

Compound Words with Vowel Digraphs

 Read the words in each box. Draw a line between the two words that will make a compound word. Write the word on the line.

1.	2.	3.
cook ● ● break	hide ● ● line	saw ● ● line
cool ● ● book	head ● ● live	sea ● ● sick
_____	_____	_____

4.	5.	6.
pea ● ● not	truth ● ● pick	foot ● ● stool
ped ● ● nut	tooth ● ● pack	cool ● ● book
_____	_____	_____

 Write two sentences using some of these compound words.

1. _____

_____

2. _____

_____

 Help your child tell a story that uses all the compound words on this page.

Read this poem. Talk about the questions at the end.

in daddy's arms I am tall

& close to the sun & warm

in daddy's arms

I can see over the fence out back

I can touch the bottom leaves on the big magnolia tree

in Cousin Sukie's yard

in daddy's arms

in my daddy's arms the moon is close
closer at night time when I can almost touch it
when it grins back at me from the wide twinkling skies

in daddy's arms I am tall
taller than Benny & my friends Ade & George
taller than Uncle Billy
& best of all
I am eye-ball-even-steven with my big brother Jamal

in my daddy's arms

I am strong & dark like him & laughing

happier than the circus clowns

with red painted grins

when daddy spins me round & round

& the whole world is crazy upside down

I am big and strong & proud like him

in daddy's arms

my daddy

—Folami Abiade

Think & Talk What does the child in this poem think of his dad?
How do you know?

I Am Happy, I Am Sad

 Write three words that mean *happy*. Write three words that mean *sad*.

happy

_____

_____

_____

sad

_____

_____

_____

▶ **Write a sentence about something that makes you happy and something that makes you sad.**

1. I am happy when

_____.

2. I am sad when

_____.

 With your child, talk about what makes you happy and what makes you sad. Write a poem together about things that make you both happy.

Read the words in each line. Circle the word that is used twice. Write it on the line.

every   again   please   together

1. every   even   every   _____

2. again   always   again   _____

3. plums   please   please   _____

4. together   together   tomatoes   _____

 Write the best Star Word from above on the line in each sentence. Use each word only once.

5. "Can I _____ get a new toy?" the boy asked his dad.

6. Janie and Yuka went to the park _____.

7. I _____ go for a run when the sun is shining.

8. Karl wanted to read the same story _____.

 Have your child read sentences 5-8 to you. Together, think of original sentences that use *every, again, please,* and *together.*

Star Words: *every, again, please, together*

 Write the best Star Word on the line in each sentence.

every **again** **please** **together**

1. I smile _____ time I see my little kitten.

2. Anna hit the ball and then she hit it _____.

3. My little sister says "_____" every time she asks for help.

4. Karl wanted to read the same story _____.

5. The puppy wagged his tail _____.

6. My mom gives me an apple for lunch _____ day.

7. Jack and Bing like to sit _____ on the bus.

Write two sentences. Use the Star Words *every, again, please,* and *together*.

1. _____

_____

2. _____

_____

Suffixes *-ful* and *-less*

Add *-ful* and *-less* to the base word. Write the new words. Read the new words.

	-ful	-less
1. care	_____	_____
2. harm	_____	_____
3. hope	_____	_____
4. help	_____	_____
5. power	_____	_____

Read the red words. Make words that end in *-ful* or *-less*. Write the words you make on the lines.

full of cheer   1. My Uncle Jack is _____.

had no clouds   2. The sky was _____.

with many colors   3. The clown wore a _____ costume.

had no spots   4. Sally's shirt was _____.

always helping us   5. Our teachers are very _____.

With your child, make up sentences using the words in items 1–5. Use this as a model: *I am **careful** when . . . ; I am **careless** when . . .*

Review Suffixes

 Read the sentences. Write the base word for the red word in each sentence.

1. My aunt Joan is very forgetful. _____

2. Kittens can move quickly. _____

3. We had a restful evening at my
   uncle's house.

   _____

4. The careless child spilled the paint.

   _____

5. The king lived happily ever after. _____

6. That bug is harmless. _____

7. Sung was thankful for the gift. _____

8. The boy gladly helped his little sister. _____

9. The game was scoreless. _____

 Help your child read the red words to you and give examples of things that fall into that category, for example, restful: quiet music, a good book, etc.

Vowel Diphthongs *oi* and *oy*

Write consonants, blends, and digraphs on the lines to make words.

-oy	**-oil**
_____**oy**	_____**oil**
_____**oy**	_____**oil**
_____**oy**	_____**oil**

Circle the word that completes the sentence. Write it on the line.

boy coins	1. That _____ has lots of _____.
toy point	2. I will _____ to the _____ on the table.
moist soil	3. The _____ is _____ after the rain.
enjoy voyage	4. I hope you _____ your _____ on the boat.

Vowel Diphthongs *oi* and *oy*

 Say each picture's name. Fill in *oi* or *oy* to make a word. Read the words.

1.

b_____

2.

___c___n___

3.

___enj_____

4.

___b___l___

5.

_____t_____

6.

___p___nt___

Have your child read the words on this page to you.
Help your child write them in alphabetical order.

Draw a line from each picture to the words that describe it.

1.  ●

● a wise owl

2.  ●

● a black and white cow

3. ●

● a gold crown

 Read the words in the box. Write the best word in each sentence.

| town | down | fowl | now | plowed |

4. Mom said, "Come here _____!"

5. Nancy ran _____ the hill.

6. A hen is one kind of _____.

7. We live in a busy _____.

8. The farmer _____ the field.

Two Sounds of *ow*

 Read the words in the box. Sort them by vowel sound. Write the words on the lines.

brown gown grow howl know
owl own show throw wow

COW

_____

_____

_____

_____

_____

crow

_____

_____

_____

_____

_____

Write a sentence using some of these words.

_____

_____.

Vowel Diphthong *ou*

 Draw a line from each picture to the words that describe it.

1.  ●

● a sour apple

2. ●

● a hound's mouth

3.  ●

● a loud shout

 Read the words in the box. Write the best word in each sentence.

found	Ouch	loud	mound	south

4. The truck made a _____ noise.

5. The train left at 10 o'clock and headed _____.

6. Jack _____ a penny on the ground.

7. When I hurt my leg, I yelled, "_____!"

8. The ant climbed to the top of the _____.

Three Sounds of *ou*

▶ **Read the words in the box. Sort them by vowel sound. Write the words on the lines.**

cloud	double	group	mouse	spout
trouble	you	young	youth	

soup

_____

_____

house

_____

_____

touch

_____

_____

▶ **Write a sentence using some of these words.**

_____

_____ .

Have your child read his or her original sentence to you. Together, create more sentences using words from the word sort.

Vowel Pair *ew*

 Read the words in the box. Write the best word in each sentence.

blew   flew   grew   knew   new   threw

1. Today I fly my kite; yesterday I _____ it.

2. Today I throw my ball; yesterday I _____ it.

3. Today I grow; yesterday I _____.

4. Today I know; yesterday I _____.

5. Today the wind blows; yesterday it _____.

6. Today my toy is old; last year it was _____.

 Read the words in the box. Write the best word in each line. You will use one word twice.

blew   chew   few   grew

Andrew had a _____ coins. He got

a pack of gum to _____.

He _____ a bubble. The bubble

_____ and _____. At last

it went POP! Andrew has gum all over his face!

Review Vowel Diphthongs

> Say each picture's name. Write *oi*, *oy*, *ow*, or *ou* to make a word. Read the words.

1. h __ se	2.  cl __ n	3.  b __
4.  br __ n	5.  b __ l	6.  c __ ns
7.  c __ ch	8.  __ l	9.  cl __ ds
10.  c __ s	11.  t __ s	12.  p __ nt

City Mouse and Country Mouse: A Play

 Read this play. Talk about the question at the end.

Narrator: *Country Mouse lived in the country. His cousin lived in the city.*

Country Mouse: I love the country! The air is so fresh. It is nice and quiet. But I get lonely sometimes. I think I will invite my cousin from the city to visit me. It will be a nice change for her. I will send her an e-mail.

Dear Cousin,
Please come to the country. I would love to see you again.
Your cousin,
Country Mouse

City Mouse: A visit to the country-what a good idea! I would like to visit the country. It would be good to relax.

Narrator: *City Mouse went to the country to visit her cousin.*

Country Mouse: How nice to see you! Let me show you where you will sleep. Then we will go out to the field to gather dinner. We will find delicious seeds and roots.

City Mouse: What? You have to gather your own dinner? You eat seeds and roots? In the city, I have lots of delicious food in the house where I live. It's there waiting for me. I don't like to hunt for food. I don't think I will stay here very long.

Country Mouse: I'm sorry. I always go out to gather food.

City Mouse: Come to the city and stay with me. I will show you the good life.

Narrator: *The next day, Country Mouse went with his cousin to the city. When they got there, they were very hungry.*

Country Mouse: I'm hungry. Let's eat!

City Mouse: Come to the kitchen. Look at all that bread.

Narrator: *Just as they were going to take a bite, the cook walked in the door.*

City Mouse: Run! We can't let the cook catch us.

Country Mouse: Why not?

City Mouse: If the cook catches us, she will sweep us away. Let's go the basement. There is better food there.

Narrator: *City Mouse and Country Mouse went into the basement.*

City Mouse: Look at all that meat. We will have a good meal here.

Country Mouse: OK. Let's eat!

Narrator: *Just as they were going to take a bite, they heard a loud MEOW.*

150   Lesson 71

Country Mouse: What's that?

City Mouse: That's Max, the cat. Run as fast as you can! If he catches us, he will eat us! Follow me to the cheese room.

Narrator: *City Mouse and Country Mouse ran to the cheese room.*

Country Mouse: Wow! Look at all that cheese! I've never seen as much cheese. I want some of that yellow cheese.

City Mouse: Stop! That box is a trap. You can't eat that cheese. If you try, the trap will close and you will be caught.

Country Mouse: Wait a minute! You have all this delicious food. But you can't eat it. The cook and the cat and the trap keep you away. I'm going back to the country where I can eat good food in peace.

Narrator: *And he did.*

 What do you think is the lesson of this story?

> Read the words in the box. Write each word next to its meaning.

country	lonely	invite	relax
delicious	gather	hungry	basement

1. _____ the part of a house below the ground

2. _____ land with farms and small towns; land outside a city

3. _____ very good to eat

4. _____ collect things; bring things together into one place

5. _____ wanting food; needing something to eat

6. _____ without someone else

7. _____ rest from work

8. _____ to ask someone to visit you

 With your child, use these words in original sentences.

City Mouse and Country Mouse: Story Writing

 Write your own story. Make notes here.

Title: City Mouse and Country Mouse

Characters: City Mouse, Country Mouse, Max, the cook

Setting: City house and country field; a long time ago

Plot: Country Mouse invites City Mouse to visit. City Mouse doesn't like the country and gets her cousin to come to the city where life is better. Country Mouse finds the city dangerous and comes home.

My Title: _____

My Characters: _____

My Setting: _____

My Plot: _____

_____

_____

_____

_____

Parent Letter

Dear Parents,

Your child is beginning the final unit in *Phonics Plus* Book B. Coming to the end of second grade is another milestone in your child's education, a time to celebrate all that your child has learned this year and to look ahead.

With your help, your child has learned a lot about letters and sounds, folk and fairy tales, trains, and other topics. Your child is learning more and more words and becoming a better and better reader. What you do at home—reading with your child, talking about school, pointing out words in your kitchen and at the supermarket—remains very important to your child's learning. You should also keep doing the *Phonics Plus* exercises designed for you and your child to do together.

Your help is especially important during the summer months when your child is out of school. During the summer, children have lots of free time. Make sure that some of this time is used for reading. During the summer, you can:

- *Get a reading list from the school or library.* Your child's teacher or local librarian can suggest which books would be good reading for your child over the summer.

- *Set aside some time for reading every day.* This could be a time to settle down after lunch or before dinner.

- *Balance reading with television.* When your child asks, "Can I watch TV?" make a deal that equal (or at least some) time be spent reading. Your child might discover that the characters who live in the pages of books are more interesting than those who live on the TV screen.

- *Challenge your child* to read all the books in a series (like *Henry and Mudge,* for example) or all the books by a particular author (like Peggy Parish). Your child can become an expert on these books.

- *Have your child keep a diary or journal* of summer activities. Your child can write about each day's activities before going to bed each evening. You can write responses if your child doesn't mind sharing.

- *Keep reading to your child.* Share stories, poems, and information books that you and your child have enjoyed all year.

The more your child reads during the summer, the more he or she will avoid the "summer slump" that often causes reading levels to slip. Summer reading gives your child a boost for third grade.

Sincerely,

John F. Savage

Carta a los Padres

Queridos padres:

Su hijo/hija está comenzando la última unidad de *Phonics Plus* Book B (Libro B). Aproximarse al final del segundo grado es otra meta importante en su educación, un tiempo para celebrar todo lo que ha aprendido este año y para mirar hacia adelante.

Con su ayuda, su hijo/hija ha aprendido mucho acerca de las letras y los sonidos, cuentos populares y de hadas, de trenes y de otros temas. Aprende palabras nuevas continuamente y cada vez lee mejor. Lo que hacen en casa (leer juntos, conversar de lo que hizo en la escuela, señalar palabras en la cocina y en el supermercado) sigue siendo muy importante para su aprendizaje. También debería ayudarle haciendo juntos los ejercicios de *Phonics Plus* diseñados para hacer en casa.

Su ayuda es especialmente importante durante los meses de verano, cuando su hijo/hija no va a la escuela. Asegúrese de que se utiliza parte de este tiempo para leer. Otras formas en el verano de ayudar son:

- *Obteniendo una lista de lecturas en la escuela o en la biblioteca.* El maestro/la maestra o un bibliotecario/bibliotecaria pueden recomendarle libros adecuados para que su hijo/hija lea durante el verano.

- *Reservando tiempo para leer cada día.* Este tiempo se puede dejar después del almuerzo o antes de la cena.

- *Buscando un equilibrio entre la lectura y el televisor.* Cuando le pregunte, "¿Puedo ver televisión?", convénzale de que debe dedicar el mismo tiempo (o al menos un tiempo) a leer.

- *Provocando a su hijo/hija* a leer todos los libros de una serie (como *Pablo Diablo, El pez arco iris* o *Kika Superbruja,* por ejemplo) o todos los libros de un autor determinado (como Hans Christian Andersen).

- *Haciendo que lleve un diario* de sus actividades veraniegas. Puede escribir acerca de sus actividades diarias antes de acostarse cada noche. Usted puede escribir comentarios si a él o ella no le importa mostrarle su trabajo.

- *Leyendo a su hijo/hija.* Compartan los cuentos, los poemas y los libros informativos con los que disfrutaron juntos todo el año.

Cuanto más lea durante el verano, menos posibilidades habrá de que se produzca el "olvido veraniego" que a menudo perjudica los niveles de lectura. La lectura durante el verano refuerza el aprendizaje para el tercer grado.

Atentamente,

John F. Savage

Read this story. Talk about the question.

Long ago, when the world was new, the sky was very dark. No stars shone at night.

People worked hard. They grew corn to eat. They kept their corn in a big bin behind the house of the Great Chief.

One day, the people of the village found that their corn had been stolen. The lid had been pushed off the bin and corn was scattered on the ground.

"Who would steal our corn?" the people asked. The next night, the people hid. They watched their corn bin. A big Spirit Dog with sparks of light came from the woods. Spirit Dog tipped the lid off the bin, ate some corn, and ran away. The people were frightened.

They went to Wise Woman. "What can we do?" they asked Wise Woman.

"Gather your drums and rattles," Wise Woman told them. "We will wait for this Spirit Dog. When he comes, we will make a great noise and frighten him away."

That night, all the people in the village hid. Spirit Dog appeared and began to eat the corn. Wise Woman shouted "NOW!" and the people made a noise as loud as thunder.

When Spirit Dog heard the noise, he was so frightened that he ran across the field. Corn was spilling from his mouth. He ran to the top of a high hill and leaped into the sky. He ran across the sky so that the people could not see him. The grains of white corn that spilled from his mouth spread across the sky.

And that's how the stars came to be.

Think & Talk How is this story different from the earlier story *Holes in the Sky?*

Lesson 73   157

Spelling the Long *a* Sound

 Read the words in the box. Sort them by spelling pattern. Write the words on the lines.

clay	gate	rail	day	page	quake
spray	snail	name	tray	train	stain

ay

_____

_____

_____

_____

a_e

_____

_____

_____

_____

ai

_____

_____

_____

_____

Look at the model, then make your own long *a* sign. Use words from the box or your own long *a* words.

make	lake	race	trail
space	tame	snakes	save

Spelling the Long *a* Sound

**Read the words in the box. Write the best word
in each sentence.**

able	April	apron	eight
freight	great	obey	sleigh

1. When you play a game, you must _____ the rules.

2. My sister's birthday is in _____ .

3. In the winter, we ride in a _____ .

4. My dad wears an _____ whenever he cooks.

5. I have _____ fingers and two thumbs.

6. Trains carry _____ from city to city.

7. In the summer, we stay at a _____ lake.

8. Are you _____ to lift the table?

 Help your child sort the words in the box by spelling pattern (*a, ei, ea, ey*) and use them in original sentences.

Spelling the Long o Sound

 Read the words in the diamond. Sort the words by word family. Write the words on the lines.

oa

_____

_____

_____

ow

_____

_____

_____

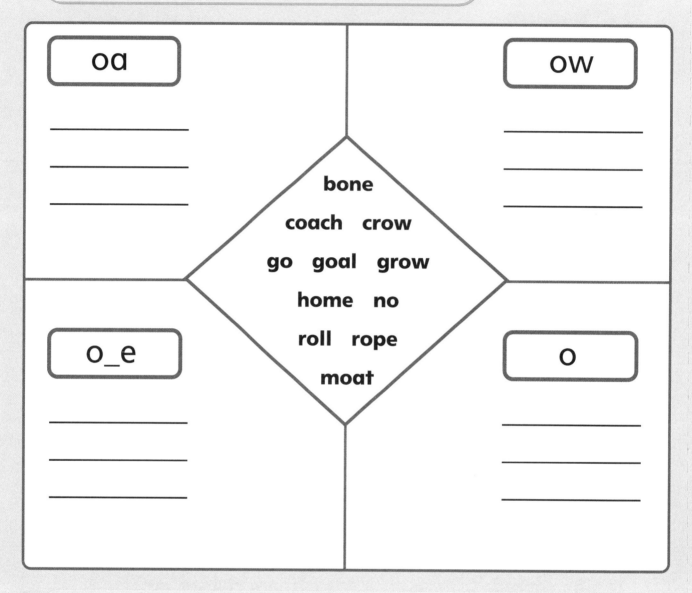

bone

coach   crow

go   goal   grow

home   no

roll   rope

moat

o_e

_____

_____

_____

o

_____

_____

_____

 Look at the model, then draw your own picture. Write a caption. Use long o words.

 Goat on a Road

_____

Spelling the Long *o* Sound

 Read the words in the box. Write the best word in each sentence.

colt   open   over   stroll   toe   told

1. The bird flew _____ the trees.

2. We went for a _____ in the park.

3. Don't step on my _____!

4. A young male horse is a _____.

5. Mr. Doe _____ a funny story.

6. It's hard to _____ this gate.

 These words have the long *o* sound but they are spelled differently. Read the words. Write the best word on each line.

hole/whole   rode/road

**road
rode**

7. We _____ the car down
the _____.

**hole
whole**

8. Joe dug the _____
_____ all by himself.

 Have your child read the sentences on this page to you. Together, make up original sentences that use *hole/whole, rode/road,* and *no/know.*

Spelling the Long *u* Sound

 Read the words in the triangle. Sort them by spelling pattern. Write the words on the lines.

u_e

ew

flew
chew
broom
flute grew
igloo June
moose mule
news prune spoon

oo

_____ _____

_____ _____

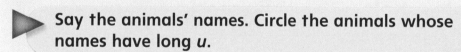 Say the animals' names. Circle the animals whose names have long *u*.

Spelling the Long *u* Sound

Read the words in the box. Write the best word on each line.

bugle	glue	music	tuba
clue	menu	uniform	

1. Luke loves to play _____. He can
   play the _____ and the _____.

2. My dad has a navy _____.

3. Bruce spilled _____ all over the table.

4. Sue found a _____ to the puzzle.

5. The lunch _____ today has pizza.

Write *to, too,* or *two* on each line. Read the text.

> **Reminder**
> Watch out for **to, too,**
> and **two.**
> **to:** in the direction of a
> place or activity.
> **too:** in addition to; also.
> **two:** 2, the number after 1.

Jen and I went _____ the circus.
We saw _____ clowns at the door.
There were lions and tigers _____.
Jen pointed _____ the roof. We
saw _____ men on swings.

Spelling the Long *i* Sound

 Read the words in the box. Sort them by word family. Write the words on the lines.

blind	find	kind	nine
child	grind	pine	whine
vine	spine	mild	wild

-ine 9

_____

_____

_____

_____

-ind

_____

_____

_____

-ild

_____

_____

Write two sentences. Use two words from the exercise above in each sentence.

1. _____

_____

2. _____

_____

Name _____

Spelling the Long *i* Sound

Read the words in the box. Write the best word in each sentence.

find	high	knight	light	right	Wild

1. The jet flew _____ in the sky.

2. Please turn off the _____ when you go out.

3. Hold up your _____ hand.

4. The _____ lived in a big castle.

5. _____ animals can be dangerous.

6. I will try to _____ your lost pen.

Write *I*, *eye*, *night*, or *knight* on each line.

Reminder
These long *i* words sound the same but have different meanings:

I	eye
night	knight

7. _____ can see you
with my _____ .

8. The _____ rode his horse
all _____ .

Spelling the Long e Sound

 Read the words in the triangle. Sort them by spelling pattern. Write the words on the lines.

ee		ea
_____		_____
_____		_____
_____		_____
_____		_____

be
cheese
cream
feed   green
he leaf me neat
queen   reach   we

e

_____   _____

_____   _____

Look at the model, then draw your own picture. Write a caption. Use long e words.

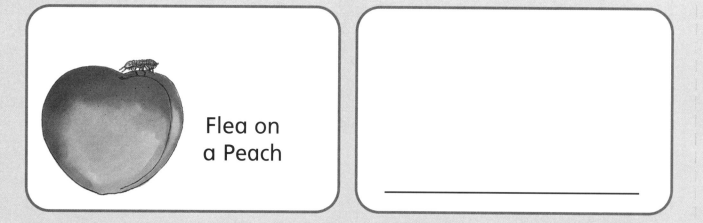

Flea on a Peach

_____

Name _____

Spelling the Long *e* Sound

▶ **Read the words in the box. Write the best word in each sentence.**

became · complete · eleven · equals · even · niece · berries

1. My _____ ate all of the _____ .

2. Five plus six _____ _____ .

3. Steve said that the job was _____ .

4. My uncle Carlos _____ a dentist.

5. The numbers 2 and 4 are _____ numbers.

▶ **Circle the word in the box that completes the sentence. Write it on the line.**

steal steel	6. That flagpole is made of _____ .
beet beat	7. We _____ the other team 2 – 1.
week weak	8. A _____ has seven days.

Have your child read the sentences on this page to you. Together, make up original sentences that use *steal/steel*, *beet/beat*, and *week/weak*.

Review Spelling Long Vowels

1.  train trane	2.  bote boat	3.  field feeld	4. 2 too two
5.  shue shoe	6.  knight knite	7.  apron aypron	8.  gole goal

Circle the word in the box that completes each sentence. Write it on the line.

hi
high

9. Clouds float _____ in the sky.

flew
flue

10. Jet planes _____ overhead.

tuba
tube

11. Steve plays the _____ in the school band.

Review Spelling Long Vowels

 Read the words in the box. Sort the words by vowel sound. Write the words on the lines.

blew	clue	cube	eve	find	grove	high
know	may	queen	rake	ride	she	so
use	team	they	tie	weigh	croak	

ā

_____

_____

_____

_____

ē

_____

_____

_____

_____

ī

_____

_____

_____

_____

ō

_____ _____

_____ _____

ū

_____ _____

_____ _____

 Write a sentence that use words from the exercise above. Use two long vowel words in your sentence.

_____

_____

r-Controlled Vowels

Say each picture's name. Write the missing letters on the lines. Read the words.

1.

p __ __ ple

2.

p __ k __

3.

c __ __ cle

4.

sc __ __ f

5.

c __ __ cus

6.

t __ __ tle

7.

h __ __ dle

8.
40
f __ __ ty

9.

__ j __ __

10.

h __ __ net

11.

p __ __ ty

12.

t __ __ get

r-Controlled Vowels in Compound Words

> Read each word. Cross out the syllable with an *r*-controlled vowel. Write the remaining syllable on the line

1. backyard  _____

2. armchair  _____

3. starfish  _____

4. forklift  _____

5. horseshoe _____

6. cornbread _____

7. birdbath _____

8. popcorn _____

Ice Cream Flavors

Read this list of ice cream flavors. Write the flavors in alphabetical order. Answer the question.

vanilla
strawberry
chocolate
peach
lemon
banana
ginger
watermelon
orange

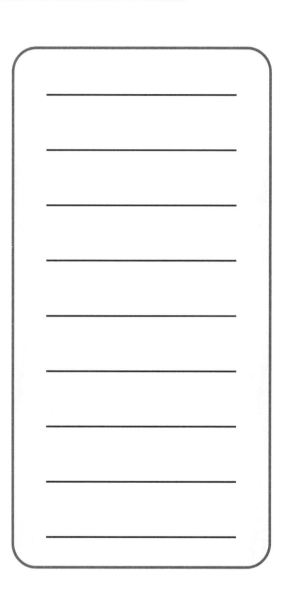

_____

_____

_____

_____

_____

_____

_____

_____

_____

What's your favorite flavor of ice cream? _____

With your child, imagine that you own an ice cream store. What flavors would you have? Write them in alphabetical order.

Name _____

Ice Cream: A Poem

> Read this poem about ice cream. Talk about the question.

Ice Cream

Ice cream, ice cream, what a treat!
Ice cream, ice cream, great to eat.

Ice cream, ice cream in a cone.
That's a treat I love to own.

Ice cream, ice cream on a stick.
That's a treat I love to lick.

Ice cream, ice cream in a dish,
A great big scoop is what I wish.

Ice cream, ice cream in my tummy.
Yummy, yummy, yummy, yummy!

Why do you think ice cream is such a popular treat?

Prefix *re-*

Reminder

The prefix re- means **again** or **back again**. To retell a story means to tell it again.

 Read each word. Add the prefix *re-* to each word. Write the new words on the lines. Read the new words.

1. draw

_____

2. spell

_____

3. pay

_____

4. check

_____

5. order

_____

6. fill

_____

 Add the prefix *re-* to the red word in each sentence. Write the new word on the line. Read the sentences.

7. My brother made his bed. I _____ it.

8. Jack named his dog Stinky. His parents _____ the dog Spot.

9. Sally opened the window. Jane _____ it.

10. I packed my backpack. I _____ it after it tipped over.

 With your child, brainstorm a list of things you did today. Restate the actions in terms of how you could redo them tomorrow (for example, rebrush teeth, redrive to school, etc.).

Name _____

Prefix *un-*

Reminder
The prefix un- has two meanings.
1. It means not.
2. It means reverse or undo an action.

 Read each word. Add the prefix *un-* to each word. Write the new word on the line. Read the new words.

1. happy

_____

2. safe

_____

3. afraid

_____

4. cooked

_____

5. do

_____

6. likely

_____

 Add the prefix *un-* to the word before each sentence. Write the new word on the line. Read the sentences.

buttoned

7. I _____ my coat when I came in the door.

locked

8. Jake _____ the gate to let us in.

loaded

9. The men _____ the big truck.

folded

10. The teacher _____ the paper and read the note.

packed

11. Rosa _____ her backpack when she got to camp.

Lesson 82b

175

Read each word. Add the prefix *dis-* to each word. Write the new word on the line. Read the new words.

1. comfort

_____

2. honest

_____

3. place

_____

4. please

_____

5. order

_____

6. like

_____

Add the prefix *dis-* to the word before each sentence. Write the new word on the line. Read the sentences.

connect 7. Dad will _____ the plug.

obey 8. Lin's sister might _____ the babysitter.

appear 9. The clown made the ring _____.

agree 10. I _____ with what you think.

With your child, make up sentences using the words in items 1-6.

Name _____

Prefix *in-*

Read each word. Add the prefix *in-* to each word. Write the new words on the lines. Read the new words.

1. correct _____

2. active _____

3. complete _____

Write the best word from above in each sentence.

4. The volcano was _____ for years.

5. The teacher told me that my answer was _____.

6. The jigsaw puzzle with the missing pieces is _____.

Draw a line from the correct prefix to the base word.

in ●
    ●perfect
im ●

in ●
    ●mature
im ●

in ●
    ●possible
im ●

Draw a line from each prefix to a base word to make new words. Read the new words. Write the best word on each line. Read the sentences.

un ●   ● draw
re ●   ● correct
in ●   ● happy

I was _____ when the teacher

told me to _____ the picture

because it was _____ .

---

un ●   ● pleased
re ●   ● placed
dis ●   ● cooked

The cook _____ the _____ meat

because we were _____ with it.

---

im ●   ● lock
un ●   ● possible
in ●   ● visible

It was _____ to _____ the door

because it was _____ .

Word Building with Prefixes and Suffixes

 Build new words with *like* and *care*. Use prefixes and suffixes. Build three new words with each base word. Write your words on the lines.

Prefixes	Base Words	Suffixes
un- dis-	like care	-s -ed -ing -ly -less -ful

1. _____   4. _____

2. _____   5. _____

3. _____   6. _____

Write two sentences with the words you made.

1. _____

_____

2. _____

_____

Days of the Week

> Read the names of the days of the week. Answer the questions.

Sunday   Monday   Tuesday   Wednesday   Thursday   Friday   Saturday

1. The first day of the week is _____.

2. The last day of the week is _____.

3. The first school day of the week is _____.

4. The last school day of the week is _____.

5. The day that comes after Monday is _____.

6. The day in the middle of the week is _____.

7. The day that comes before Friday is _____.

8. My favorite day of the week is _____ because _____ _____ _____.

Look at a calendar with your child. Talk about things you usually do on certain days of the weeks and during certain months of the year.

Months of the Year

> Read the names of the months of the year.
> Answer the questions.

January	**April**	**July**	**October**
February	**May**	**August**	**November**
March	**June**	**September**	**December**

1. What is the first month of the year? _____

2. What three months have only one syllable?
   _____, _____, and
   _____

3. Which month begins with the letter *O*? _____

4. What months are summer in the U.S.? _____,
   _____ and _____

5. Which month comes right before December?
   _____

6. What month begins with the letter *S*? _____

7. Which month usually has 28 days? _____

8. What is the last month of the year? _____

9. What month is not listed here? _____

Multisyllabic Words with Consonant Blends

 Say each picture's name. Write the first two letters of each word. Read the word. Circle the number of syllables in the word.

1.

_____ ocodile

2   3

2.

_____ actor

2   3

3.

_____ orkel

2   3

4.

_____ arinet

2   3

5.

_____ amingo

2   3

6.

_____ etzel

2   3

7.

_____ aceship

2   3

8.

_____ ippers

2   3

9.

_____ opwatch

2   3

 Have your child use each of the words on this page in a sentence.

Words with Three-Letter Blends

 Read the words in the diamond. Sort the words by spelling pattern. Write the words on the lines.

scr		spr
_____		_____
_____	**screaming**	_____
_____	**spraying splinter**	_____
	struggle splendid	
	streaming sprinkle	
	scrapbook straining	
spl	**splatter sprout**	str
_____	**scratching**	_____
_____		_____
_____		_____

 Write two sentences. Use two words from the exercise in each sentence.

1. _____

   _____

2. _____

   _____

Multisyllabic Words with Consonant Digraphs

 Read the words in the box. Write each word next to its definition.

> **chimpanzee   chipmunk   chocolate   shadow**
> **shelter   thunder   whirlpool   whisper**

_____ 1. water spinning quickly around

_____ 2. a loud noise you hear during
                      a storm

_____ 3. dark, sweet candy

_____ 4. a place that protects animals
                      and people

_____ 5. to speak in a low, soft voice

_____ 6. dark shape made by blocking light

_____ 7. small, brown, furry animal with
                      stripes on its back

_____ 8. a kind of ape

Word Puzzle

Say the names of the pictures. Write the pictures' names in the boxes.
Write the mystery word on the line at the bottom of the page.

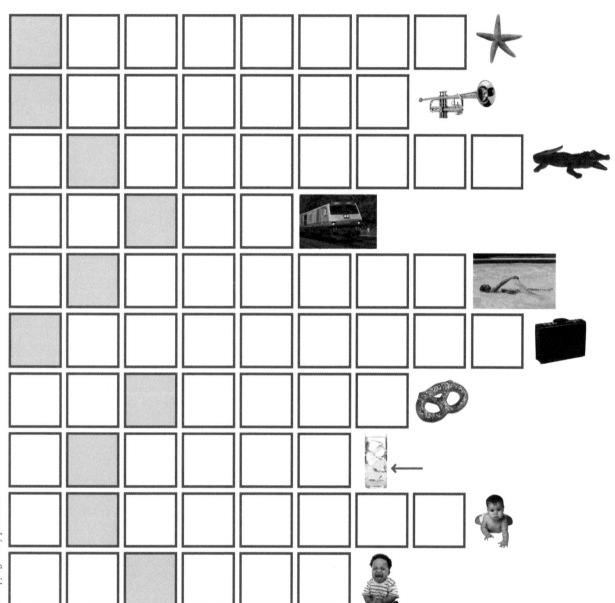

The mystery word is: _____

 Help your child make a puzzle like this. Choose a word as your "mystery word," then fill in other words around it.

Read the words in the box. Write the best word in each sentence.

enough	**nephew**	**night**	**pharoah**
phonics	**saxophone**	**sight**	

1. Sam is Uncle Ralph's _____ .

2. A _____ was a ruler in old Egypt.

3. We learn _____ to help us read.

4. The children had _____ candy at the party.

5. Phil plays the _____ really well.

6. The sky at _____ is a beautiful
_____ .

 Help your child give definitions for the words on this page and use them in sentences.

Consonant Digraphs *kn* and *wr*

 Write *kn* on the lines, then draw a line from each word to the picture.

kn

___ee___ •   • *(knife)*

___ife___ •   •

 Write *wr* on the lines, then draw a line from each word to the picture.

wr

___eath___ •   • *(wreath)*

___ap___ •   •

 Write a sentence. Use as many *kn* and *wr* words as you can.

_____

_____

Read these poems. Circle all the homophones.
Talk about the questions.

Renee Wright

Renee Wright was very bright.

She could read and she could write.

Her mistakes were out of sight

'Cause everything she wrote was right.

Two Gnus with Shoes

I knew a gnu who wore a shoe

    And he said that the shoe was new.

And then I met another gnu

    And he said that he wore one too.

I can't believe two gnus I knew

    Were smart enough to wear a shoe.

 Which of these two poems did you like best? Why?

Read these poems
with your child.

Consonant Combinations *mb*, *tch*, and *dge*

> Say each pictures name. Complete each word with *dge* or *tch*. Read the words you make.

1. ju_____	2. wa_____	3. bri_____
4. ba_____	5. ca_____	6. ma_____

> Read the words in the box. Write the best word in each sentence.

bridge   lamb   porridge   thumb

1. Mary had a little _____ whose fleece was white as snow.

2. Jack Horner put in his _____ and pulled out a plum.

3. The three billy goats crossed the _____ .

4. Goldilocks ate the _____ of the three bears.

Circle the word that belongs in the space. Then write the word on the line. Read the sentences.

1. Mom made a _____ of chocolate
   batch   patch
   _____.
   fridge   fudge

2. The little _____ _____how to fly.
   wren   wrap   knob   knew

3. We put a _____ over the _____
   write   wreath   knock   knob
   on the door.

4. Don't go too near the _____ of the
   ears   edge
   _____.
   ledge   lodge

5. The hikers _____ to the top of the
   trudged   judged
   _____.
   ranch   ridge

6. A tiny _____ bit me on the
   gnat   knot
   _____.
   watch   wrist

7. The teacher _____ the _____ on
   wrong   wrote   alphabet   elephant
   the board.

With your child, make up sentences that use the pairs of green words, for example, *I put the fudge in the fridge.*

Name _____

Celebrate with Humor

 **Read these knock-knock jokes with a partner.
Write your own joke on the lines.**

Knock knock.
Who's there?
Boo.
Boo who?
You don't have to cry about it!

Knock knock.
Who's there?
Ken.
Ken who?
Ken I come in?

Knock knock.
Who's there?
Sue.
Sue who?
Surprise!!!

Knock knock.
Who's there?
Liz.
Liz who?
Liz go out together.

Knock knock.
Who's there?
Ben.
Ben who?
Ben a long time!

Knock knock.
Who's there?

_____
_____
_____ who?
_____
_____

Read this story to see what happened to Silly Jack. Talk about the questions at the end of the story.

Jack and his mother lived in a small house in a small town. One Sunday, Jack's mother said, "I work hard at my job. I think you should find a job, too."

So on Monday, Jack went to work on a farm. At the end of the day, the farmer gave Jack a pot of butter. Jack put the butter in his pocket and walked home. When Jack got home, the butter had melted.

"Silly Jack," said his mother. "You don't carry butter in your pocket. You should have wrapped the butter in cloth and put it in a bucket of cold water."

On Tuesday, the farmer gave Jack a bag of salt. Jack wrapped the salt in cloth and put it in a bucket of cold water. When Jack got home, the salt was gone.

"Silly Jack," said his mother. "You don't carry salt in cold water. You should have put the salt in a bag."

On Wednesday, the farmer gave Jack a cat. Jack put the cat in a bag. The cat scratched and screamed. It tore the bag and ran away. When Jack got home, the cat was gone.

"Silly Jack," said his mother. "You don't put a cat in a bag. You should have carried it in a basket."

On Thursday, the farmer gave Jack a shovel. Jack put the shovel in a basket, but the basket was too small and the shovel fell out. When Jack got home, the shovel was gone.

"Silly Jack," said his mother. "You don't put a shovel in a basket. You should have put the shovel on your shoulder and carried it home."

On Friday, the farmer gave Jack a donkey. Jack put the donkey on his shoulder and started to carry it home.

On his way home, Jack passed the king's palace. The princess in the palace was very sad. She never smiled or laughed. "My daughter is so sad!" said the king. "The person who can make the princess laugh shall have a job at the castle."

On Friday, the princess looked out the window and saw Jack carrying a donkey on his shoulder. "That is the funniest thing I have ever seen," the princess said. She smiled and then she began to laugh.

"You made the princess laugh, "the king told Jack. "You can have a good job at the castle. You can be a jester. It will be your job to make the princess laugh every day."

Jack was happy with his new job.

Think & Talk What do you think Jack will do to make the princess laugh?

Silly Jack: Story Writing

Write your own story. Make notes here like the sample below.
Write your story on a separate sheet of paper.

Title: Silly Jack

Characters: Silly Jack, his mother, the princess, the king

Setting: a small town, a castle

Plot: Silly Jack works on a farm, but has a hard time bringing home his pay. At the end, he gets a job at a castle.

My Title: _____

My Characters: _____

My Setting: _____

My Plot: _____

_____

_____

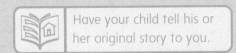
Have your child tell his or her original story to you.

▶ **Read the words to this song. Sing the song.**

She'll be coming 'round the mountain when she comes,
She'll be coming 'round the mountain when she comes,
She'll be coming 'round the mountain, she'll be coming
'round the mountain
She'll be coming 'round the mountain when she comes.

Oh, we'll all go out to greet her when she comes,
Oh, we'll all go out to greet her when she comes,
Oh, we'll all go out to greet her, oh, we'll all go
out to greet her
Yes, we'll all go out to greet her when she comes.

Sing this song
with your child.

Name _____

▶ **Read the words to this song. Sing the song.**

Down by the station early in the morning
See the little pufferbellies all in a row.
See the engine driver pull the little handle,
Chug, chug, toot, toot, off we go!

Lesson 92b

197

Celebrate with Information: Trains

 Read this text about trains. Talk about the question.

Whoo, whooooooo! Whoo, whooooooooo! Trains carry people and goods all over the land. Day and night, night and day, trains work hard.

Trains are pulled by powerful engines called locomotives. The first locomotives were steam engines. They were run by wood or coal. Then came more powerful diesel engines. These engines pulled longer and longer trains.

Some diesel engines are still used. Today, most trains today run by electricity. Subway trains are electric trains. Modern high-speed trains -bullet trains-can carry people at speeds of over 100 miles per hour.

People ride on passenger trains. The train pulls into the station and the conductor yells, "All aboard!" Most passenger trains carry people short distances very quickly. Other passenger trains carry people long distances. On these trains, people can eat and sleep.

Freight trains carry heavy loads. These trains are so heavy that they often need more than one engine to pull them. Freight trains have many types of cars:

- Boxcars to carry cargo like clothes and computers.
- Flatcars to carry big items like trailers and machines.
- Hopper cars to carry grain and coal.
- Refrigerator cars to keep food cold.
- Tank cars that carry liquids like milk and juice.

The caboose is the last car on the train. It is for the people who work on the train.

Cars and airplanes have changed the way we travel. But trains are still important to our lives.

 How do trains help us every day?

Read the words in the box. Write the words on the diagram.

runs on tracks

has cars for eating and sleeping

pulled by a locomotive

bullet trains

has boxcars and flat cars

carries goods like cars and clothes

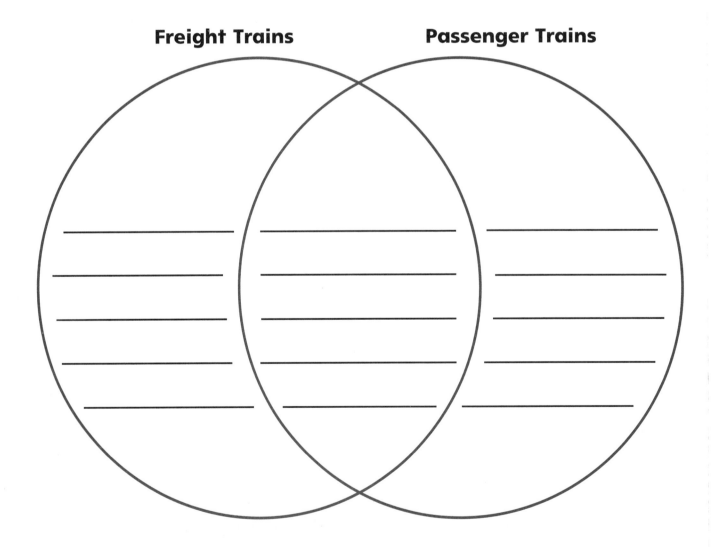

Freight Trains

Passenger Trains

Find out what else your child knows about trains. Go to the library together and look for more information to add to the diagram.